Alternatives to Prison

Contemporary Issues Series

1 Tariq Ali (ed.): *New Revolutionaries: Left Opposition*
2 A. B. Downing (ed.): *Euthanasia and the Right to Death: The Case for Voluntary Euthanasia*
3 Keith Hindell and Madeleine Simms: *Abortion Law Reformed*
4 Geoffrey Spyer: *Architect and Community: Environmental Design in an Urban Community*
5 R. S. Morton: *Sexual Freedom and Venereal Disease*
6 Ken Coates and Tony Topham: *The New Unionism: The Case for Workers' Control*
7 Ian Henderson (ed.): *The New Poor: Anatomy of Underprivilege*
8 B. H. Lee: *Divorce Law Reform in England*
9 J. E. Hall Williams: *Changing Prisons*
10 Roy Wallis (ed.): *Sectarianism: Analyses of Religious and Non-Religious Sects*
11 John A. Loraine: *Syndromes of the Seventies: Population, Sex and Social Change*
12 Tom O'Carroll: *Paedophilia: The Radical Case*
13 Gillian E. Hanscombe and Jackie Forster: *Rocking the Cradle: Lesbian Mothers: A Challenge in Family Living*
14 Stephen Stanley and Mary Baginsky: *Alternatives to Prison: An Examination of Non-Custodial Sentencing of Offenders*

Stephen Stanley and Mary Baginsky

Alternatives to Prison

AN EXAMINATION OF NON-CUSTODIAL SENTENCING OF OFFENDERS

PETER OWEN · LONDON AND WASHINGTON DC

Cloth edition ISBN 0 7206 0522 9
Paperback edition ISBN 0 7206 0626 8

PETER OWEN PUBLISHERS
73 Kenway Road London SW5 0RE

First published 1984

Printed in Great Britain by
Photobooks (Bristol) Ltd

Contents

Preface

The history of this book deserves some elucidation. Mary Baginsky produced the initial manuscript, but was unfortunately unable to complete it. It fell to me subsequently to revise and finish her work. I would like therefore to record my thanks to Mary, without whose contribution this book would not have been begun. In the course of rewriting and updating, I have necessarily made substantial changes to the original, both in style and content. Thanks go to Meg Lewis, who typed my draft of the manuscript, and also to my colleagues in the Inner London Probation Service who have read the manuscript, or parts of it. I am grateful for their comments but wish to stress that the resultant work is my own responsibility and does not represent the policies of ILPS. Finally, I would like to thank my secretary Dorda O'Hanlon for her assistance with some revisions and, most importantly of all, my wife Suzanne for all her patience and forbearance while this book was being written.

Stephen Stanley

Chapter One

THE CASE AGAINST PRISON

The English prison system is in a crisis. This is now an accepted fact, asserted almost daily by journalists, MPs, pressure groups, individuals working within prisons and the organizations which represent them, and accepted, tacitly or overtly, by the Prison Department and even by the Home Secretary himself.

There is an equal degree of agreement about the immediate cause of this crisis: overcrowding. Prisons in England and Wales contain about 44,000 inmates in buildings designed for less than 39,000. The consequences of such overcrowding are manifold. As more and more prisoners are crammed into often decrepit and outdated buildings, the physical conditions of their imprisonment become increasingly appalling and, to quote the report of the prison inspectors on Gloucester Prison (published in February 1982), 'the quality of life for prisoners . . . becomes degraded to the point of being squalid'.

One obvious solution to the problem would be to build more prisons to house the ever-growing population of prisoners. There are many theoretical and philosophical objections to such an approach, and it is also inordinately expensive. A report by NACRO, the National Association for the Care and Resettlement of Offenders, published in 1981,[1] demonstrated that spending on prisons had already increased two and a half times as fast as public expenditure over the preceding twenty-five years, and that in 1979/80 the average cost of keeping one person in gaol for a year was £7,110 (only £400 less than the average salary of a working man). Furthermore, as the director of NACRO, Vivien Stern, pointed out in January 1982, costs had been kept to this level only 'by imposing an intolerable degree of overcrowding and allowing the physical conditions of many establishments to deteriorate to an alarming degree'.

NACRO's opinion that 'only a substantial reduction in the prison population will prevent the prison service from consuming an even larger share of public expenditure in the years ahead'[2] was shared by the former Home Secretary Mr William Whitelaw (now Lord Whitelaw). In February 1982 he stated that 'the prospects for reducing or eliminating overcrowding . . . are dependent on a substantial reduction in the overall prison population'. This approach was also favoured by the Prison Officers' Association, who wanted to see some offenders diverted from prison and given alternative sentences. Their plea, reported in the *Daily Telegraph* of 1 December, 1981, was accompanied by a chilling warning that British gaols would erupt into 'mutiny and violence on an American scale unless urgent action is taken to solve overcrowding and poor conditions'.

At the time of going to press, however, it appears that the incarceration of prisoners has a higher priority in the policies of the present Home Secretary, Mr Leon Brittan. On 21 November, 1983, he announced that the Government were embarking on a 'programme of new prison building [that] far surpasses anything undertaken before in this century'. Fourteen new prisons are planned, at an estimated cost of £246.2 million, providing 10,600 new prison places by 1991. According to Mr Brittan, the allocation of additional resources to the Prison Service was 'a landmark in the long-term strategy of this government to provide an effective, efficient and civilized' penal system. It must be said, however, that to date extra spending on prisons has been more than overtaken by a rise in the number sent there. As Andrew Rutherford remarked in *The Times*, 'The real danger is that Mr Brittan's prison-building programme will send a signal to decision-makers throughout the criminal justice system that additional capacity is available.'[3] There is no evidence that increased spending will provide a long-term solution to the problem of overcrowding.

Britain's prisons are not only overcrowded, they also do not fulfil one of their prime tasks, to stop people offending.

The sentencing of offenders can be said to have three main objectives:

to punish the offender for committing a crime;

to reform the offender so that he is unlikely to reoffend;

to deter others from offending and the offender from doing wrong again.

To these may be added a fourth objective: to protect society by taking the offender out of circulation, the so-called 'incapacitation effect'.

These objectives of punishment, reform and deterrence are not new. In Europe, the doctrine of punishment by the state for wrongdoing appears to stem from Roman and Byzantine law. Well-articulated ideas of reform and deterrence are much more recent, but they are at least as old as the prison system in Britain. Thus the 1779

Act of Parliament authorizing the building of state prisons envisaged that this 'might be the means under providence, not only of deterring others from the commission of like crimes, but also of reforming the individuals and inuring them to the habits of industry'.

While the conditions in British prisons seem nothing short of punishing, prisons have demonstrably failed to reform or deter offenders. A Home Office study of the reconviction of a sample of offenders convicted in 1971[4] found that 71 per cent of males given a custodial sentence in that year had reoffended within six years, and about 60 per cent within three years, *of their sentence*. A further analysis of these findings showed that, except in the case of first offenders, men sent to prison were as likely to be reconvicted as men with similar records who were given other sentences* for similar offences.[5]

If prisons are so bad and so ineffective, why do we have them and why are they so overcrowded?

It is our contention that many of those sent to prison could, and should, instead be given one of the various non-custodial sentences now available to the courts. We intend to show that it would be no worse for our society if more offenders were diverted from prison. In proposing this, we find ourselves in the company of (among many others) the Prison Officers' Association and a number of prison governors. The problem is that, while there may be wide agreement between workers in the criminal justice system and reformers of different degrees that the courts' use of prison sentences should be restrained, there is much less agreement about what alternatives to custody should be used and how far they should replace prisons. For this reason it is necessary to look at each kind of alternative in detail, before we come to a more general discussion of their role and impact.

We must also recognize that prisons have survived in this society for three reasons: inertia, the philosophy of treatment, and because they seem to be needed.

It is perhaps worth exploring these in some detail. To take the last first, it is an observable fact that many reformers accept that there are some offenders who must be kept in prison, because they present a threat to society or because the offences of which they have been convicted are so serious that prison is the only suitable sentence to punish them and to deter others.

Thus Robert Kilroy-Silk, Labour MP for Ormskirk, tabled in

* For the sake of clarity, all the ways courts can deal with convicted offenders are called 'sentences' in this book, although some of them are technically 'disposals' which may obviate a formal sentence.

January 1982 an amendment to the then Criminal Justice Bill to make the imprisonment of rapists mandatory (except for mentally abnormal offenders, who would be committed to a special hospital) when, as the law stood, sentencers had the power *not* to impose a prison sentence. Yet at about the same time Mr Kilroy-Silk was calling also for a restriction in the use of custodial sentences for juvenile offenders.

These two attitudes are not incompatible, and indeed they demonstrate a more logical approach to sentencing than does official policy, but they do illustrate that for many people there are certain limits which the promotion of alternatives should not overstep. Thus the social and political interpretations of particular offences play a large part in delineating the discussion of alternative sentences and help to reserve some prison places, as it were, for certain kinds of offenders.

The second bastion of prisons has been the philosophy of treatment. The idea that criminals exhibit pathological symptoms which can be treated depends on a belief that social behaviour can be explained by psychological and physiological laws. Those whose behaviour is deviant can be identified as having certain personal characteristics 'causing' that behaviour, and treatment – so the argument runs – will reduce or remove those characteristics or their effects. This belief led on to the idea that a spell in prison could and should be constructive, an idea that has a history of two centuries or more. The British prison building programme of the late eighteenth century was one of many to be justified in part by the supposed reformative benefits of the regime adopted, be it solitary meditation, evangelical exhortation, the provision of work or 'training', or participation in group therapy. Such treatment has been seen as being good in itself, which leads to the argument that, as it is good, then the greater the benefit will be the more the treatment is applied. The general effect has been to provide a rationale for relatively long, or even indeterminate, custodial sentences, so that prisons really will be able to reform their inmates.

In recent years, the working ideology of English prisons has retreated a long way, under the pressure of numbers, from treatment to containment. Nevertheless, English prisons still keep much of the language of training and classification and still subscribe to what Howard Gill describes as the 'sacred cow' that the job of prison staff is rehabilitative in intent. And the *idea* of treatment in custodial institutions, despite the lack of proof that it is a valid one, is still there, perhaps waiting to be resurrected if the immediate crisis ever passes.

It seems to be important that any demonstration of the value of alternatives to prison should place treatment *in* prisons in its proper perspective. The idea of treatment is perhaps the only *positive* contribution the prison system can make to dealing with offenders; otherwise its role is almost purely negative – stopping, in one way or another, people from committing criminal acts or exacting the State's retribution for these acts. We would hope that recognition of this would help to promote the use of non-custodial sentences, which can be more beneficial to the offender and are certainly less destructive.

Such aspirations, however, run up against the most effective prop of the system, its inertia. The prison system and the sentencing policies which support it plough on virtually unmoved by attempts at reform. For example, the new non-custodial alternatives introduced by legislation of the late 1960s and early 1970s have had, as we shall see, less decisive effects on sentencing than was hoped, because they appear not to have been used exclusively as alternatives to custody.

We must also recognize that this inertia is reflected in public attitudes to crime and punishment. A survey on this subject, carried out by National Opinion Polls for *The Observer*[6] in March 1982, while demonstrating a wide degree of public support for giving non-custodial sentences to non-violent offenders who now go to prison, also showed that the most favoured Government response to prison overcrowding would be to build more prisons (preferred by about half the respondents in the survey) as opposed to reducing the number of inmates (preferred by a third of those interviewed).

The Observer presented these results as a response to the then current concern of the 'law-and-order lobby' that the Government was 'soft' on crime, and argued that the figures showed public opinion to be more moderate and more in favour of non-custodial sentencing than many politicians believed. It is also worth noting that those questioned in the survey felt that crimes against people, and particularly crimes of violence, were more deserving of prison sentences than were crimes against property, while the law tends to be more weighted against the latter offences.

Nevertheless, although there may be more rationality in people's views about the sentencing of offenders than may be apparent in official and judicial policy and practice, the fact that offences such as burglary and vandalism still attracted substantial minorities in favour of, or not opposed to, custodial penalties (47 per cent for burglary, 35 per cent for vandalism), suggests that the sentencers themselves still lead rather than lag behind public opinion. For example, in 1981 just over one-third of convicted male burglars received an immediate custodial sentence.[7] Certainly, the expressed state of public opinion would seem unlikely to cause judges and magistrates to change their sentencing practices, and may very likely be an argument for the status quo.

It may, at this point, be helpful to outline the main custodial and non-custodial sentences available to the courts in England and Wales following the Criminal Justice Act 1982.

The type of sentence that a court can impose is determined not only by the offence, but also by the age of the offender. Offenders aged under 21 cannot be sent to prison, but can be sent to youth custody or detention centres. Those aged 21 or over can only be sent to prison. Similarly, while probation orders are reserved for those aged 17 or over, and community service orders for offenders over the age of 15, juveniles can be given a care order or a supervision order (if they are aged between 14 and 16) or an attendance centre order. Finally, there is a group of sentences, including fines, conditional and absolute discharges, which can be used for any age group.

These variations in sentencing options appear to stem from two causes. The first is the historical development of a separate jurisdiction, and therefore of distinctive sentences, for juveniles. The second, and related cause, is the ideology of treatment.

We have already observed that the idea that prisons can 'treat' offenders, as doctors 'treat' patients, has helped to justify their existence; belief in the value of treatment also structures the sentencing of offenders. All sentences (except an absolute discharge) are punitive in that they impose some kind of restriction or obligation on the offender – be it to spend time in custody, to pay a fine, to report to a probation officer or to refrain from reoffending under threat of further punishment. In so far as they are immediately punitive, or carry the threat of harsher punishment, all these sentences may have some hypothetically deterrent effect, although the general existence of such an effect has not been proved.[8]

Some measures, however, are also designated as reformative, in that they will hopefully induce a change in the recipient which makes him less likely to reoffend. These sentences are particularly plentiful for younger offenders: care orders, supervision orders and youth custody for the under-17s; probation orders and youth custody for those aged 17–20. Furthermore, the Prison Department has its own treatment-oriented establishments for adults, 'training prisons', which it has tried to protect from the evils of overcrowding (at the expense of conditions in the older local prisons).

Finally, there is the institution of after-care, the provision of support to ex-inmates of custodial institutions to resettle them in the community (and thus to undo some of the damage done by their incarceration). This is available to all ex-prisoners, but is compulsory for parolees and particularly, in this context, for all those under the age of twenty-one who have served a custodial sentence.

Having looked at the nature of the crisis in Britain's prisons and at the ideas underpinning the system, we must next consider its mechanics. How, and why, are people sent to prison?

First of all it is worth noting that a significant minority of the prison population have not in fact been convicted of a criminal offence. Of the 44,000 inmates of English prisons, about 5,000 are on remand, awaiting trial; 2,000 are awaiting sentence and a further 400 are described as 'non-criminal prisoners'.[9] Indeed, of over 500,000 defendants (of all ages) charged with an indictable offence in 1981, between 40,000 and 50,000 were remanded in custody at some stage in the court proceedings.[10] Of the 465,000 *sentenced* for indictable offences (that is to say, charges where defendants can choose trial by jury at the Crown Court instead of summary trial by the magistrates; all indictable offences are punishable, in theory, by a custodial sentence of six months or more), 69,000 (15 per cent) received immediate custodial sentences and a further 34,000 received suspended sentences of imprisonment. Of the 69,000 immediate custodial sentences, 39,000 (56 per cent) were imposed by the Crown Court and 30,000 (44 per cent) by magistrates' courts.

Overall, just over half of those sentenced by judges of the Crown Court received an immediate custodial sentence, while at magistrates' courts, which have more limited powers of sentencing, one in thirteen of those sentenced for indictable offences went to prison or detention centre.

In addition, magistrates' courts committed 13,000 offenders to the Crown Court for sentence, of whom 9,000 received an immediate custodial sentence; these account for nearly a quarter of the custodial sentences imposed by the Crown Court. In 1981 magistrates' courts also imposed about 5,000 immediate custodial sentences on offenders found guilty of summary offences where the maximum punishment was six months or less in custody.

Finally, about 17,000 people each year are sent to prison for defaulting on fines.

The average prison sentence imposed in 1981 was about ten months.

While magistrates' courts are directly responsible for about two-fifths of custodial sentences, and, through heavy fines, remands in custody and committals for trial and sentence, are indirectly responsible for at least two-thirds of those who spend any time in custody before or after conviction for sentence, the great majority of the prison population at any one time have come through the Crown Court, because Crown Court sentences are longer than those imposed by magistrates' courts (who cannot impose a custodial sentence longer than six months). This fact may have implications for the further development of alternatives. A reduction in the use of custody by magistrates' courts will have a lesser effect on the prison population than will any reduction in its use by the Crown Court. By contrast a shift in Crown Court sentencing could have in the long term a disproportionate effect on overcrowding in prisons.

TABLE I

Custodial Sentences (for All Offences) in 1981: by Type of Court

	Magistrates' Courts	*Crown Court*	*All Courts*
Detention Centre	11,100 (17%)	2,900 (4%)	14,000 (21%)
Borstal Training	–	8,800 (13%)	8,800 (13%)
Immediate Custodial Sentences (Total)	24,200 (37%)	27,600 (42%)	51,800 (79%)
Sentence of (up to):			
6 months and under	24,200 (37%)	9,900 (15%)	34,100 (52%)
Over 6 months and up to 12 months	–	6,500 (10%)	6,500 (10%)
Over 12 months and up to 2 years	–	6,400 (10%)	6,400 (10%)
Over 2 years and up to 4 years	–	3,600 (5%)	3,600 (5%)
Over 4 years	–	1,200 (2%)	1,200 (2%)
Total Custodial Sentences	35,300 (54%)	30,500 (46%)	65,800 (100%)

Source: *Criminal Statistics, England and Wales 1981*, HMSO, London, Cmnd 8668.

Note: Since the implementation in May 1983 of the relevant parts of the Criminal Justice Act 1982, sentences of borstal training (and prison sentences for young offenders) have been replaced by sentences of youth custody. Magistrates' courts may sentence offenders to periods of up to six months in youth custody.

Table I shows how custodial sentences for both indictable and summary offences in 1981 were distributed by type of court and by the type and length of the sentence. We have already noted the magistrates' courts' contribution to the prison population, but it is also noteworthy that, if we include sentences to borstals and detention centres (now short youth custody and detention sentences), short sentences of under 12 months account for 83 per cent of the custodial sentences imposed. Indeed, while the number of custodial sentences made has risen since 1973, the average length of prison sentences has tended to decline slightly, from 3.8 months to 3 months for sentences imposed in magistrates' courts and from 20.9 months to 16.6 months for Crown Court sentences. The prison population of 44,000, however, includes about 17,000 who will be in prison for a year or more – nearly half those actually serving a custodial sentence.* Thus any long-term move towards emptying the prisons must cover this group.

Hypothetically a number of strategies are available to cut down the prison population. These fall into two groups: reducing the number of custodial sentences and shortening their lengths. The 1979–83 Tory Government appeared to be committed to strategies of the second kind: for example, the abortive proposal for supervised release of short-term prisoners; the partially suspended sentence and the availability of determinate sentences for young offenders as set out in the Criminal Justice Act. In theory such ideas are not without merit and indeed without some such action it seems unlikely that the prison population will be contained. We will discuss these strategies further in Chapter 6, but for now it is sufficient to observe that they are also liable to encourage sentencers to use shorter custodial sentences more often.

For this reason those strategies aimed at reducing the numbers of custodial sentences made seem to us to have more potential. These can be divided into three groups:

alternative sentences for imprisonable offences;

statutory limitations on the use of custody;

diversion from sentencing.

There are already a variety of non-custodial sentences available to courts, as Table II shows. These sentences can be described according to whether the offenders are supervised during them (usually by the

* These include all prisoners (adult and young) sentenced to eighteen months and over. Those receiving shorter sentences, or sent to borstal or detention centre, would have served less than a year in an institution.

TABLE II

Non-Custodial Sentences

Offender's Age	*With Supervision*	*Without Supervision*
10 – 13	Money Payment Supervision Order Supervision Order Attendance Centre Order Care Order	Conditional Discharge Fine
14 – 16	Money Payment Supervision Order Supervision Order Attendance Centre Order Care Order Community Service Order*	Conditional Discharge Fine
17 or over	Money Payment Supervision Order Probation Order Community Service Order Suspended Sentence Supervision Order	Conditional Discharge Fine Suspended Sentence

* For offenders aged 16.

probation or social services), as with a probation or community service order, or not, as with a conditional discharge. (Fines and suspended sentences can have, as the Table shows, supervision orders attached.)

As with custodial sentences, so their alternatives, and particularly the supervisory ones, are structured by the age of the offender. Those under 17 are subject to different supervisory orders with different conditions and resources than are older offenders.

A fourth dimension, not shown in the Table, is the distinction between older and newer non-custodial sentences. In the late 1960s and the 1970s the primacy of fines and probation as the alternatives to custody was challenged by the introduction of new supervisory sentences for juvenile offenders (care and supervision orders) and of new sentences – the suspended prison sentence and the community service order – designed specifically as alternatives to prison.

We shall discuss the use of alternative sentences in Chapters 2–5, dealing respectively with non-custodial sentences for juveniles, the development of probation and the short history of the newer schemes.

The strategy of limiting by statute the use of custodial sentences for some types of offenders and offences has two strands. The first can be seen in the ways that mentally disturbed, handicapped or abnormal offenders may be sentenced by the courts. Here the law recognizes that some individuals need particular kinds of treatment and care which are justified by their mental condition alone, and not necessarily by their offence. The extent to which offenders in these groups should be dealt with according to the tenets of a criminal justice system, or by other criteria, is a complex issue and one that we shall attempt to tackle in Chapter 7.

The second strand to the strategy of limitation is the identification of certain offences as not meriting custodial sentences. In the last few years the Home Office has directed a considerable amount of attention to the problem of 'persistent petty offenders' who are imprisoned mainly on charges of drunkenness and vagrancy, with the aim of removing them from the prison system by providing alternative resources or by restricting courts' powers to sentence them. Similarly, the Criminal Justice Act 1982 ended imprisonment for soliciting by prostitutes.

This kind of strategy depends on two elements, identifying the offence as not meriting a custodial sentence, and identifying the offender as one who will not be deterred or be restrained by any realistic custodial sentence. We discuss this further in Chapter 7.

The strategy of diversion is one that is foreign to English law, although much used in the USA. Essentially it consists of identifying offenders (who are prepared to admit their guilt) who can be helped through a 'diversionary programme' or who will in some way make reparation for their offence; if they complete the programme successfully they will not be brought to court and will not therefore be convicted of any offence. Thus administrative decisions are substituted for legal and judicial decisions.

The closest analogies to diversion in the English legal system are the abilities of the police to caution an offender instead of bringing him or her to court, and of the court to defer sentence on a convicted offender in expectation of some action or change in his or her circumstances. As police cautioning is particularly used for juveniles, we discuss this in Chapter 2, but the general issue of diversion is also raised in Chapters 8 and 9.

We should also note the fact that in several countries the prison population appears relatively lower than ours. In Chapter 8 we consider some aspects of the sentencing policies and practices that have developed in other countries, to see what lessons might profitably be learned from them.

Finally, in Chapter 9, we attempt to bring together our findings and arguments, to suggest a way for the English penal system out of the dark ages of our prisons.

NOTES AND REFERENCES

1 *NACRO Briefing: The Cost of Prison*, November 1981.

2 Ibid.

3 A. Rutherford, 'Building up a Prison Crisis', *The Times*, 25 November, 1983, p. 14.

4 G.J.O. Philpotts and L.B. Lancucki, *Previous Convictions, Sentence and Reconviction: A Statistical Study of a Sample of 5,000 Offenders Convicted in January 1971*, Home Office Research Study No. 53, London: HMSO, 1979.

5 N. Walker, D.P. Farrington and G. Tucker, 'Reconviction Rates of Adult Males after Different Sentences', *British Journal of Criminology*, Vol. 21 No. 4, 1981, pp. 357–60.

6 *The Observer*, 21 March, 1982.

7 Home Office, *Criminal Statistics, England and Wales 1981*, London: HMSO, 1982.

8 See, for example, S. Brody and R. Tarling, *Taking Offenders out of Circulation*, Home Office Research Study No. 64, London: HMSO, 1980.

9 Home Office, *Prison Statistics, England and Wales 1982*, London: HMSO, 1983.

10 Home Office, *Criminal Statistics, England and Wales 1981*, op. cit.

Chapter Two

DEPRAVED OR DEPRIVED?

The contemporary and past history of the attempts to contain, punish and treat juvenile offenders shows the confusion that lies at the heart of much criminal policy in England: are young offenders bad, or are they victims of individual or social pathologies, or of an unjust society?

The various attempts to reform the system of juvenile justice in England and Wales have suffered from our inability to answer these questions. Before the nineteenth century, children were seen more as small adults than as having special needs of their own, and the courts treated them as such, imposing penalties as severe as those used for much older offenders (for example gaol and the treadmill for stealing apples). With the Victorian 'reinvention' of childhood there began a move away from this approach, a move that was reflected in the extension of mandatory education and the imposition of restrictions of the employment of children.

Three strands can be seen in the late-nineteenth- and early-twentieth-century developments of a policy for young offenders. The first is the individual attempts at decarceration by reformers, including police court missionaries and prison governors, persuading magistrates to mitigate the savagery of their sentences. The second strand is the development of residential establishments such as reform schools and homes run by the Church of England Temperance Society as alternatives to custodial sentences or court proceedings; the third is the introduction of legislation – particularly the 1908 Children and Young Persons Act – designed to take juveniles out of the adult criminal justice system and to structure and limit the ways the courts could deal with them. Informing these changes was the growing belief that juveniles offended because of things that had happened in their background. Thus an ex-police court missionary, writing at about the turn of the century, cited home conditions as a cause of crime;[1] one of the first chroniclers of the police court mission observed that criminality might be transmitted from parents to their children and that young offenders were the victims of their environment.[2] Such arguments supported the practice of removing actual or potential offenders from their bad or non-existent homes to training schools, institutions, shelter homes or hostels. Often the children were taken into these establishments because they were *at risk* of coming before the courts, rather than because they had offended or been sentenced, and such actions – individualized 'social work' decisions – were seen as being good in themselves. (Not a view that would be applauded by the libertarians of left or right.)

The kinds of theories about the causes of and responses to juvenile offending that appeared at the turn of the century bear more than a passing similarity to those surrounding later legislation; only the context was different – the intrinsic value of 'treatment' was stressed along with a belief that the scope of such measures could and should be expanded more or less indefinitely. Thus in 1913 we find a Home Office researcher complaining, in a mirror-image of contemporary arguments, about the inadequacy of reconviction as a measure of the success of industrial schools – because too many of those for whom training had 'failed' had not been reconvicted![3]

Ideas of reform and treatment antedated the 1908 Act, but it can be seen as the first embodiment of these notions, confirming the view that a child required 'treatment' for his needs rather than punishment for his deeds. In his comments on the Act's provisions, the then Lord Advocate, Mr Shaw, said: 'The magistrate has placed before him a series of alternatives, the object being to treat these children not by way of punishing them – which is no remedy – but with a view to their reformation.' The Act established juvenile courts to deal with children under sixteen and abolished imprisonment for most offenders under this age and for all those below fourteen years of age. Following, among other things, the actions of the police court mission, and significantly in terms of what was to happen some sixty-one years later (in the Children and Young Persons Act 1969), it brought vagrant and destitute children within the jurisdiction of the courts. 1908 was also the year of the Prevention of Crime Act, which formally instituted borstal detention for young persons of fifteen and over. These borstals were intended, like the reformatory schools and industrial schools of the nineteenth century, as training grounds where offenders could be inculcated with moral values while providing them with vocational training and a severe physical regime. In effect they catered for those labelled as criminal who could no longer be sent to prison.

As a result of apparent public concern over the reported increasing rates of juvenile delinquency during the First World War the Home Office called a conference of bodies interested in the welfare of juveniles; a central committee was established and a number of Juvenile Organizations' Committees set up under the overall responsibility of the Board of Education. The central committee published a report in 1920 containing information on the home backgrounds of children who had appeared in court. The report makes depressing reading, most of the children referred to coming from emotionally and physically disadvantaged backgrounds. Its conclusions emphasized the importance of individual *treatment*, but no attempt was made to look at those children who committed offences and did not appear in court. It is important to remember that late-nineteenth- and early-twentieth-century communities operated their own social sanctions, dealing informally with many of their own offenders in their own way. Such measures usually depended on the child being known personally to the victim, to the police, or to an observer; the punishment was often swift or referred to the parents, and a court appearance was rarely in question. So it was the children without what we now call a 'supportive family', or those on the fringes of the community for one reason or another who tended to come into contact with the criminal processes, who were seen by the reformers as the main problem and whose experiences and needs helped to guide the development of the juvenile justice system.

Influential during the 1920s was Cyril Burt's study *The Young Delinquent* (a work which antedates those where his methodology and conclusions appear to be, at best, highly suspect).[4] Working from a relatively small sample, Burt demonstrated that there was a link between poverty and delinquency, in that a significantly high proportion of his delinquents came from poor or very poor families, but that delinquency also depended on the home environment. The largest group in his sample – 42 per cent – came from 'comfortable' artisan and skilled working-class families, but, as he pointed out, 'In the better kind of home, the parents and interested friends more often desire – and more successfully attempt – to debar their children's petty misdemeanours from becoming the subject of official inquiry and action: the official agency in its turn, when appraised of all the facts, is more reluctant to banish a child from a good home to an industrial school.'

Children from so-called 'comfortable' homes were not the only ones to be diverted from the criminal justice system. Many of the popular social histories written about such areas as the East End of London or the dock areas of Liverpool and Glasgow in the early decades of this century contain accounts of juvenile encounters with the police and other adults in which community or familial sanctions were imposed.

Burt's work had a strong influence on Home Office thinking at the time, and may be seen as another step towards a re-evaluation of the relative responsibilities of welfare and criminal justice agencies.

Perhaps the decisive legislative step came with the Children and Young Persons Act 1933, which made it possible to commit a child or young person who had committed an offence to the care of the local authority in much the same way as a child or young person in need of care and protection. A local authority could refuse such an order (and frequently did so), but for the first time it was possible in law to treat a child offender in the same way as a deprived child; thus reliance on the initiatives of charitable workers was reduced.

The Second World War prompted a further movement. The years between 1939 and 1945 had highlighted some of the problems of children who were not brought up by their parents. Mass evacuation of children from the large cities was a matter of public attention, especially the problems faced by children adjusting to a new environment after being deprived of their own homes. It was against this background that the Curtis Committee sat in 1945 and accepted in its terms of reference the deprived child supported by public assistance, the child on a fit person order and children in approved schools, remand homes and other institutions where a child may spend a period of his life, but excluded from its considerations 'all questions concerned with the operation of the penal code, and . . . the conditions in Borstal institutions'.[5] The Curtis Committee's terms of reference thus set an arbitrary boundary between approved schools, remand homes and probation hostels on the one hand, and borstals (as subject to the penal code) on the other.

The Committee accepted the evidence of the Home Office that 'it is often an accident whether a child is brought before the court for an offence or as a neglected child, and it is accordingly appropriate that the same methods of treatment should be equally available in either case'.[6] This recommendation was supported by the evidence given by other bodies, and the final report of the Committee, combined with growing pressure from various sources, opened the way for a comprehensive service for the care of all children living in a particular area. With the establishment of the children's departments by the Children's Act 1944, the responsibility for remand homes, the organization and part of the finance of approved schools, supervision orders and fit persons orders, as well as the care of children in need, passed to one local authority body. But, at the same time, there was being implemented the Criminal Justice Act 1948, which abolished imprisonment and corporal punishment for young people under seventeen years old and introduced specific penal measures aimed at dealing with delinquency: detention centres[7] and attendance centres.[8]

Thus while the methods of handling 'delinquents' and 'the rest' remained, in part, still distinct, there had been a considerable move away from the earlier position of treating child offenders in much the same way as adult offenders. Delinquency was increasingly regarded as a result of deprivation. This change of attitude was less marked, however, towards offenders aged fifteen or over. They found themselves in a sort of half-way house between adult offenders on the one hand and deprived children on the other. For those aged 17–20 the courts had limited powers of imprisonment (sentences of under 6 months or over 18 months) or recourse to borstals, which were seen as reformative (hence the phrase 'period of borstal training'), or detention centres (primarily punitive at first) as alternative custodial measures. For the fifteen- and sixteen-year-olds imprisonment was not available (although long-term detention for serious offences was), but the courts could make use of detention centres and borstals.

The post-war structure of custodial penalties and sanctions suggests a spectrum of emphases on care (suitable for younger offenders and deprived children) and control and punishment (for older offenders). Embedded in this pudding was the sometime 'plum' of borstals, set up primarily to provide treatment (training) over an indeterminate period, but used increasingly by magistrates as a mid-range sentence – more serious than detention centre, less serious than a long prison sentence. For treatment and care in the community the options of care orders or (for children aged fourteen or over) probation orders were available.

In the generation following the Second World War Governments regarded delinquency as caused by poor social and family environments, and increasingly looked to the social services (rather than the criminal justice system) to remove or reduce its causes. Thus, in 1949, a joint circular was sent from the Home Office (which until 1971 was responsible for children's departments in local authorities) and the Ministry of Education urging local authorities to consider ways of preventing delinquency; the causes listed included 'unsatisfactory home conditions, bad and overcrowded housing, family conflicts, neglect, lack of affection and parental interest'. The joint circular issued by the Home Office and the Ministries of Education and Health in the following year drew attention to children neglected or ill-treated in their own homes and urged the social services to co-ordinate their actions in such a way as to avoid, wherever possible, removing children from their homes. Both these circulars, together with one issued in 1953 by the Home Office and Ministry of Education, recognized the need for action at an early stage to avoid the deterioration of a family which may lead to child deprivation and subsequently to delinquency. In these circulars, the growing emphasis on keeping families together and children in their own homes is noteworthy. By this time earlier ideas on delinquency had been modified by Bowlby's[9] views (now less accepted) of the importance of constant parenting adults in a child's early life. Removal from home, so often used by early reformers, was seen as a last resort and the focus of intervention turned increasingly towards the family.

In 1960 the Committee on Children and Young Persons, under the chairmanship of Lord Ingleby, sat to consider juvenile courts, remand homes, approved schools and neglected or ill-treated children. Its Report[10] criticized most severely the lack of co-ordination in the social services and, taking up the themes of the Government circulars, stressed that the way to prevent delinquency was to help families who were in need. A number of the Committee's recommendations were incorporated into the Children and Young Persons Act 1963 and the responsibility for implementing this Act was given to the children's departments of the local authorities, who were also, in theory, given powers and financial resources to keep families together.

By 1963 the fate of a young offender depended on a number of considerations which governed whether or not he should appear before a court; for example, the policy of local police towards cautioning offenders, the activity of the social services (and particularly the children's department) in the area, the kind of school the child attended, professional assessments of parental attitudes and responsibility and, not least, the degree to which 'delinquency' was contained and controlled within the family. In some instances the appearance of a child or young person in court occurred only after a series of consultations by the police with other parties involved, but more often the previous policy of non-consultation and autonomous action by the police continued.

The development of the 'welfare-orientated' model of dealing with young offenders coincided with the growth of the idea of a unified social service as the value of social work intervention and treatment in dealing with the problems of all individuals, including offenders, was promoted.

In April 1964 the Labour Party Research Department published a report, *Crime, a Challenge to Us All*,[11] that envisaged a Family Service which would be the umbrella body dealing with the numerous aspects of child welfare and would attempt to ensure the promotion of the 'health, happiness and well-being of the whole family as an effective way of preventing delinquency'. This report provided the essence of the White Paper *The Child, the Family and the Young Offender*[12] which, when published in August 1965, stated that 'much delinquency and indeed many other social problems can be traced back to inadequacy or breakdown in the family. The right place to begin, therefore, is with the family' (para. 5). The White Paper's proposal to establish family courts to replace juvenile courts met with fierce opposition and was quickly abandoned, but the similar juvenile panels proposed for Scotland by the Kilbrandon Report[13] were implemented in the Social Work (Scotland) Act 1968. The 1968 White Paper *Children in Trouble*[14] again showed a theoretical commitment to the multicausal nature of delinquency:

> Frequently it is no more than an incident in the pattern of a child's normal development. But sometimes it is a response to unsatisfactory family or social circumstances, a result of boredom in and out of school, an indication of maladjustment or immaturity, or a symptom of a deviant, damaged or abnormal personality. (para. 6)

Combined with this was a more sophisticated treatment model than had previously been advanced. The emphasis was on the treatment and care of children who have needs, with the act of committing an offence seen as a symptom of a general need. This White Paper was the basis for the Children and Young Persons Act 1969.

The Act made a number of important changes. The following summary lists its main provisions, followed by an indication of how each provision was – or was not – implemented.

S1. For all offenders under fourteen and for many over that age, juvenile court proceedings were to be civil rather than criminal; it would be necessary to prove not only that an offence had been committed but also that the child was in need of care and control which he/she would not receive without a court order. (Although the use of the 'offence' condition as an alternative to prosecution has been possible since 1971, it is very rarely used.)

S4. No child under the age of fourteen was to be charged with an offence (with the exception of homicide). (The age has not been raised from ten.)

S5. Care proceedings were to be available to limit prosecutions, and this would be facilitated by compulsory consultations between local authority officers and the police, except where a qualified informant (a member of the police force) decided that this would be inappropriate. (Such consultations are not yet compulsory, which means that, in most cases, the police influence is paramount in decisions about which juveniles will be prosecuted and which ones will be cautioned.)

S12. Although the term 'Intermediate Treatment' (which appears in the 1968 White Paper) was not mentioned specifically in the legislation, the Act established the framework by which it would be possible for juvenile courts when making a supervision order to vest in the social worker or probation officer (who would be supervising the child or young person) the authority to require that child to attend specified places and be involved in specified activities for a defined period of time. (The first Regional Intermediate Treatment Scheme was introduced in July 1973.)

S13. Supervision orders were to replace probation orders for offenders under seventeen years of age, with social workers normally dealing with those under the age of fourteen and probation officers dealing with those over that age. (In operation.) Provision was also made for a gradual transfer of responsibility for all supervision orders on older offenders to social services departments. (This has happened only to a limited extent, and then only by negotiation by individual probation areas and social services departments.)

S20. Approved school orders and fit person orders were to be replaced by care orders whereby juveniles would be committed to the care of the local authority who would decide whether to place them in a residential establishment or return them home. (This came into operation on 1 January, 1971.)

Other Provisions

The separate designations of approved schools, remand homes, reception centres and children's homes were abolished and the homes brought into one system of 'community homes'. The decision as to which type of home the juvenile would be placed in would be vested in the local authority. (Implemented.)

Attendance centres were to be phased out. (They continue to exist.)

Detention centres were to be phased out for juvenile offenders and replaced by residential requirements to supervision orders. (Detention centres continue to exist.)

The minimum age for sentence to borstal training would be raised from fifteen to seventeen years of age. (The age at which this could be imposed remained at fifteen.)

The 1969 Act represented a whole-hearted step towards the identification of juvenile offenders with deprived children, and a commitment to *treating* them in the same ways and in the same institutions. Thus while the juvenile courts were still to decide on guilt or innocence, the responsibility for deciding how and where a child made subject to a care order would be placed was vested in professional social workers. The implementation of the Act, by the 1970–74 Conservative administration, showed, however, a retreat from this position: custodial and punitive measures remained accessible to the juvenile courts, and the complete integration of non-custodial supervision and treatment of children remained unachieved, responsibilities instead being shared, to varying extents, between the probation service and the social services departments. Morris[15] points out, however, that, despite the loss of key sections, the Act could have been implemented *informally* by the police, the courts and the probation and social services, had they had the will or resources to do so. As it was, even some of the sections that were implemented had only minimal effects.

Problems were also encountered with the operation of the Act. Its introduction (on 1 January, 1971) virtually coincided with the implementation of the Social Services Act, setting up, from 1 April, 1971, social services departments embracing the functions of the former children's, mental health and welfare departments of local authorities. As the children's departments had been the most 'professional' of the three, many of their best staff were promoted out of the field into managerial posts, and a considerable amount of direct experience of working with children was lost. The new social services departments were also faced with the responsibility for implementing the 1970 Chronically Sick and Disabled Persons Act – a task which could of itself have consumed the total resources available to them.

A brief bid for growth, at an average rate of 10 per cent a year, encouraged by the then Secretary of State for Social Services, Sir Keith Joseph, collapsed in the face of the Government's financial crisis of 1973 and finally, in 1974, the reorganization of local authorities (outside London) disrupted or disorganized many departments.

In this maelstrom, it is perhaps not surprising that the new direction shown by the 1969 Act was followed only haltingly by social services departments, and with hindsight its inadequacies can be attributed at least in part to the problems of, and lack of resources for, its implementation.

It can also be argued, however, that the Act was fundamentally misconceived. Its assumptions rested on two foundations: that juvenile delinquency was a product of poor home circumstances, and that individual treatment, administered by social workers, could act to remove this cause (if the child remained at home) or to mitigate its effects (if the child was placed elsewhere). The claims made for 'treatment' in the 1960s, however, proved to be over-optimistic, resting as they did on a relatively inadequate basis of research which had in fact already begun to show[16] that treatment might not meet the objectives that legislators had in mind. Furthermore, the Act in effect replaced arbitrary judicial decisions about the disposal of young offenders with often equally arbitrary bureaucratized decisions. These operated particularly in two spheres: firstly the Act increased the use of cautioning by the police to divert young offenders from appearing before the courts; and secondly decisions about the placement of young offenders subject to care orders were given over to social workers, on the basis that the placement reflected 'need' and not at all the court's assessment of the seriousness of the offence or the appropriateness of punishment.

Yet, as implemented, the Act *failed* to reduce the courts' powers to imprison young offenders (as the relevant sections were not implemented and the courts appeared unwilling or unable to restrain themselves), and it also failed to decriminalize juvenile delinquency (because the minimum age at which a person could be charged with an offence was *not* raised, and because a residual power not to use criminal proceedings was ignored by the courts).

Finally, these defects were compounded by the fiction, or belief, that the custodial measures available (directly or indirectly) to the juvenile courts were themselves directed towards the *treatment* of offenders. Thus borstals and detention centres remained, as if for those who had 'graduated' from the care system without benefiting from its treatments. The community homes themselves have the power to reject any child considered to be 'unruly' or 'difficult'. (Section 31 of the Act, although rarely used, provided that unruly juveniles over the age of 15 could be referred back to the juvenile courts for further disposal.)

It is in fact difficult to discern what the effects of the Act have been on the sentencing, treatment or criminality of juveniles. The number of reported offences has continued to rise since the implementation of the Act (it was rising before), as has the number of juveniles cautioned by the police or found guilty by the courts – from 92,000 in 1965 to 164,000 in 1979, a rise of 78 per cent at a time when the juvenile population in general rose by 19 per cent, and the number aged 14–16 (those most at risk of being cautioned or convicted) grew by 25 per cent. Over the decade 1969–79, however, the number of findings of guilt recorded by the juvenile courts rose by *only 6 per cent*, so the apparent juvenile crime wave had dwindled to a few ripples.[17]

The explanation for these phenomena is the massive growth in the police use of cautioning for young offenders (or rather for certain types of young offender). In 1965, for every juvenile cautioned by the police, three were sentenced by the courts; by 1979 this ratio had fallen to one to one, and the number of juveniles cautioned had virtually quadrupled.

The particular criteria used by the police in deciding whether or not to caution a person rather than bring him or her before the courts vary between police forces, but the following are a constant minimum without which no caution can be administered:

> the person cautioned must be demonstrably guilty of the offence as charged (in other words the police must be confident that they would get a conviction if the case came to court);
>
> the person cautioned must admit the offence and he/she (or his/her parent or guardian) must consent to the caution (and can therefore choose a court hearing);
>
> the victim of the offence must consent to leave the matter to the police.

The widely different rates of police cautioning of juveniles suggest that there is considerable scope for interpretation of these rules; some police areas will caution a juvenile once only, with a second offence resulting in a juvenile court appearance, while others may allow two or more cautions before charging a juvenile with an offence. Factors such as the previous records of other juveniles involved in the offence, or the police perceptions of the juvenile's home circumstances, will also affect the police decision to caution.

It can be seen that the process of cautioning rests a great deal on the *judgement* of the police as to how they use their discretion. With juveniles, the police are expected to liaise with the local social services department and probation service (if appropriate) before deciding whether to caution or to prosecute an individual.[18] Although in practice these liaison schemes vary in quality and the role of social services may only be as providers of information, there is evidence[19] that in some police areas the decision whether or not to caution is based in part on 'social judgements' – whether the child is 'sorry'; whether his or her home circumstances are 'good' – related to the ideas of deprivation or poor parenting as causes of delinquency. Children from relatively more stable or less poor families may be more likely to be cautioned, while children from broken homes, from large, poor families and (indirectly) from ethnic minorities[20] are more likely to come before the courts.

Police cautioning can be defended because relatively few of those juveniles (20 per cent of first offenders) who are cautioned subsequently reoffend. This may be because the police are 'weeding out' the best risks among the known offenders and leaving the worse risks, those in 'need', and the recidivists to be dealt with by the courts;

nevertheless, police cautioning, by acting as an alternative to prosecution, can act as an alternative to custody.

This kind of argument can, however, be criticized on several grounds. Firstly, those cautioned are, by the nature of the process, those least at risk of a custodial sentence, or of being placed in a community home.

Secondly, the protagonists of labelling theory would argue, the process of cautioning is less likely to produce reoffenders than is the process of trial and sentence in a court, irrespective of the individuals involved. Indeed, this argument is supported by empirical evidence.[21]

Thirdly, the process of cautioning sets up stereotypes of juveniles who are suitable or unsuitable. If you happen to conform to the wrong stereotypes – to be, for example, one of several children of a lone parent in a high crime area – then your chances of being cautioned are probably relatively low. Thus cautioning tends to work against the ends of justice in a system which attempts, for juveniles, to balance justice against need.

In addition, the statistics show that the growth of police cautioning has been accompanied by a growth in the courts' use of custodial sentences, and a reduction in their use of non-custodial sentences. Thus cautioning, if it is related to these trends, appears to have supplanted the latter sentence rather than the former, and particularly to have replaced supervision orders.

It is received wisdom that the growth in police cautioning has diverted many juveniles from court proceedings, but it is at least possible that it has also brought into the system many who would previously have been dealt with informally.[22]

There are two kinds of evidence in support of this view. Firstly, if cautioning diverted the 'low-risk' delinquents from the courts, then one might expect to see a relationship between the cautioning rate in an area and the use of custodial sentences by the local juvenile courts (areas with high cautioning rates would have courts with high rates of custodial sentencing for juveniles, because those suitable for non-custodial sentences had been diverted from court). In fact this relationship does not exist, as cautioning rates are *not* obviously related at all to sentencing, and its absence suggests one of the following:

that cautioning rates are related to crime rates (and therefore we would expect areas with low cautioning rates to have high rates of custodial sentencing);

that courts use custodial and non-custodial sentences in relatively constant proportions, irrespective of the types of cases or offenders before them;

that to increase the police cautioning rate above a certain level *does not* divert more offenders from the courts, but rather results in more offenders being cautioned who would otherwise have been dealt with more informally;

that cautioning rates are related to the backgrounds of those charged with offences which, in turn, may be a function of police activity.

Ditchfield[23] found that the growth in police cautioning rates in different areas was strongly associated with increases in reported juvenile crime, and this tends to support the views of Howlett[24] and Taylor[25] that many juveniles who were being referred to juvenile bureaux and cautioned would not, had these schemes not existed, have been taken before a juvenile court, and would indeed probably have been dealt with informally.

Thus we must conclude that the growth in police cautioning, even if it has diverted some juveniles from court, has not contributed to any reduction in courts' use of custody. Indeed, it is possible that it has had the reverse effect, by giving courts the impression that they are dealing with the dross of offenders while cautioning has taken the cream.

The number of juveniles sentenced to detention centre increased four-fold between 1965 and 1979, while the number placed in borstals increased ten times over the same period. Thus by the end of the first decade the operation of the 1969 Act saw a five-fold increase in the courts' use of custodial sentences for juveniles. This can hardly have been what the framers of the Act, or even the Government that introduced it, intended to happen.

Over the same period those facilities (supervision orders and care orders) aimed at securing treatment of or working with the offender in the community were squeezed out both by the growth in police cautioning and by the increasing punitiveness of the courts.

Part of the rise in the use of custodial sentences was due to a rise in the number of juveniles coming before the courts, and part perhaps to slight changes in the types of offences with which they were charged. But, overall, as the DHSS review *Offending by Young People* (1981) points out, 'the rise in custodial sentencing is caused by an increased tendency to give custodial sentences for almost all types of offence'.[26] Quite why this should be is difficult to see. There is little evidence that, despite the growth in police cautioning, the courts deal with more serious or persistent juvenile offenders than they did a decade ago.

Offending by Young People notes that over half the juveniles appearing in court were there for the first time. Of these about two-thirds received a fine or an absolute discharge; between one in four and one in five were made subject to a supervision or care order, and most of the rest got attendance centre orders, with only 2 per cent going to detention centre.

By contrast, nearly one in five of second or subsequent offenders were sent to detention centre or borstal, one in ten went to attendance centres and one in four got supervision or care orders. Furthermore, about half of those sent to detention centres and a fifth of those sentenced to borstal training had two or fewer previous convictions. So far as can be seen from the available statistics, those who went to borstal or detention centre in 1979 were likely to have had *fewer* previous convictions *but* were also *more likely* to have served a custodial sentence than were their counterparts of a decade earlier. Indeed in 1979 only 28 per cent of borstal trainees and 76 per cent of inmates of detention centres were known *not* to have served a custodial sentence already. As the DHSS report says, 'custodial sentences are sometimes used before all alternative disposals have been tried'.

There is no evidence that these trends have ceased. Thus, while only a minority of juvenile offenders receive custodial sentences, the overall picture has not been one of courts struggling to operate within the 1969 Act and only reluctantly sending persistent offenders into custody. We must also add the observation that this policy of the courts has proved singularly ineffective in deterring or otherwise diverting young offenders from further crime and convictions.

We have dealt in some detail with the weaknesses and unintended consequences of the 1969 Act because they show that well-intentioned legislation (and the Act, even cut down as it was, could still have made a contribution) is insufficient to produce a reduction in courts' use of custodial sentences. If anything, indeed, the effect has been to limit the effectiveness of care and supervision orders as alternatives to custody (grinding them, as it were, between the millstones of detention centres and police cautioning). We shall now turn to ways in which they might still be used and promoted.

Overall the numbers of care orders and supervision orders made on juvenile offenders have fallen ever since the 1969 Act was implemented; the number of care orders made following an offence fell between 1974 and 1979 from 7,400 to 4,350, and the number of supervision orders in criminal proceedings from 23,200 to 17,700 (at a time when the number of borstal and detention centre sentences rose from 4,900 to 7,000). The fall in the use of care orders was greater (40 per cent as against a 20 per cent drop in supervision orders), and this, taken with the observation that the decline in the use of supervision orders was fastest for those (aged under 14) who would be supervised by social services departments (and seldom, if ever, by the probation service), suggests that the courts remained unconvinced of the intentions and philosophy of the Act and of the ability of social services departments to meet their needs.

At the same time, the treatment of children who do come into care as a consequence of an offence has been changing. Social services departments have, by and large, become increasingly reluctant to place such children in the community home system (formerly children's homes and approved schools). Thus, whereas in the early years of the operation of the 1969 Act, social services departments saw a great need for observation and assessment centres and community homes with education (roughly the old approved schools), by 1980 the number of places available within these establishments was greater than the projected need for them; by contrast the proportion of young offenders being 'boarded out' with foster parents has been rising.

At the same time the number of *secure places* in community homes has risen (trebling in the 1970s) as a result of financial aid by Governments who hoped that the number of juveniles remanded in prisons on 'Unruly Certificates' would thereby be reduced.

The theory of care orders for juvenile offenders, and of the community home system, was that each child's needs would be assessed by social workers, who would then organize a 'placement', whether at home, with a foster parent, or in a community home, which would meet those needs. The statistics quoted above suggest a different picture – firstly that care orders have been 'squeezed' between the increases in police cautioning and courts' custodial sentencing, secondly that placements in community homes are being used relatively less often, and thirdly that the community homes used contain *more* secure places, to deal with 'unruly' children.

These trends accentuate the confusion that exists in the law's treatment of young offenders, but we must also recognize that care orders themselves are not necessarily alternatives to custody; community homes are only a step or two removed from custodial establishments, and their effectiveness is marred by their apparent inability to cope with those juveniles who are most at risk of going to detention centre or borstal.

Reoffending rates of juveniles in care are relatively lower than those sent to borstal or detention centre, but this seems to be because they are more likely to be first offenders (who are less likely to reoffend). Pat Cawson,[27] in her study of juveniles in community homes, found that reconviction rates were primarily associated with numbers of previous convictions, and that the placement in the community home was only marginally relevant. At the same time, many juveniles whose community home placements *do* break down (which may be as much the fault of the community home as of the child) may end up in custody on 'Unruly Certificates' as a result.[28]

These observations tend to dispel any beliefs that may be entertained of the absolute power of community homes to do good for all the juveniles who are sent to them. As there are limitations on their ability to reform their charges, it may be that, ultimately, the most realistic objective of the community home system is the avoidance of further harm to the child. This may seem a harsh judgement, but, as we shall see when we consider non-custodial sentences for those aged over seventeen, there are many other forms of intervention that are equally open to the same kinds of criticism – perhaps because they are so close to custodial sentences.

NOTES AND REFERENCES

1 T. Holmes, *Pictures and Problems from the London Police Courts*, London: Thomas Nelson & Sons, 1900.

2 F. Hasloch Potter, *Inasmuch: The Story of the London Police Court Mission*, London: Williams & Norgate Ltd, 1927.

3 M. Barnett, *Young Delinquents: A Study of Reformatory and Industrial Schools*, London: Methuen, 1913; quoted in R.V.G. Clarke and D.B. Cornish, *The Controlled Trial in Institutional Research – Paradigm or Pitfall for Penal Evaluators?*, Home Office Research Study No. 15, London: HMSO, 1972, p. 10.

4 C. Burt, *The Young Delinquent*, London: University of London Press, 1925.

5 *Report of the Care of Children Committee*, London: HMSO, 1946.

6 Ibid.

7 The minimum age for committal to a detention centre is fourteen. These establishments are run by the Prison Department of the Home Office and were intended as a short-term punitive sanction, lying between supervision and borstals in severity.

8 Attendance centres were intended for the 10–21 age group, to punish young offenders by depriving them of leisure time. The offender usually has to attend a centre weekly, most frequently on a Saturday afternoon, for a specified number of weeks.

9 J. Bowlby, *Child Care and the Growth of Love*, London: Penguin Books, 1953.

10 *Report of the Committee on Children and Young Persons*, London: HMSO, 1960.

11 *Crime, a Challenge to Us All*, London: Labour Party Research Department, 1964.

12 *The Child, the Family and the Young Offender*, London: HMSO, 1965.

13 *Children and Young Persons Scotland*, Edinburgh: HMSO, 1964.

14 *Children in Trouble*, London: HMSO, 1968.

15 A. Morris, 'Diversion of Juvenile Offenders from the Criminal Justice System', in N. Tutt (ed.), *Alternative Strategies for Coping with Crime*, London: Basil Blackwell and Martin Rochester, 1978.

16 See, for example, H.J. Meyer, E.E. Borgatta and W.C. Jones, *Girls at Vocational High: An Experimental Study in Social Work*, New York: Russell Sage Foundation, 1965.

17 Statistics quoted in this chapter are taken from the Department of Health and Social Services, *Offending by Young People: A Survey of Recent Trends*, London: DHSS, 1981.

18 See, for example, E.N. Goldberg and W. Warburton, *Towards Accountability in Social Work*, London: Allen & Unwin, 1977, for a brief description of the response of one area team in a local authority social services department to Juvenile Bureau referrals.

19 See D.J. West and D.P. Farrington, *Who Becomes Delinquent?*, London: Heinemann, 1973, and C.J. Fisher and R.I. Mawby, 'Juvenile Delinquency and Police Discretion in an Inner-City Area', *British Journal of Criminology*, Vol. 22, No. 1, 1982, pp. 63–75.

20 Fisher and Mawby, op. cit., suggest that direct racial discrimination (at least between whites and Asians) does not affect cautioning decisions, although it seems likely to us that police perceptions of the attitudes of members of some ethnic groups, for example West Indians, are on Fisher and Mawby's evidence likely to be effective in causing discrimination against those groups.

21 See, for example, J. Gawn, J. Mott and R. Tarling, 'Dealing with Juvenile Offenders in a New Town, 1966/67 and 1973', *Justice of the Peace*, Vol. 141, 1977, pp. 279–80; but see also D.P. Farrington and T.H. Bennet, 'Police Cautioning of Juveniles in London', *British Journal of Criminology*, Vol. 21, No. 2, 1981, pp. 123–35. This argues that the effect predicted by 'labelling theory' does not occur.

22 See A. Morris, 'Diversion of Juvenile Offenders from the Criminal Justice System', op. cit., and D.P. Farrington and T.H. Bennet, 'Police Cautioning of Juveniles in London', op. cit.

23 J.A. Ditchfield, *Police Cautioning in England and Wales*, Home Office Research Study No. 37, London: HMSO, 1976.

24 P.W. Howlett, 'Is the YSB All It's Cracked Up to Be?', *Crime and Delinquency*, Vol. 19, 1973, pp. 485–92.

25 L. Taylor, *Deviance and Society*, London: Thomas Nelson and Michael Joseph, 1971.

26 DHSS, *Offending by Young People*, op. cit., p. 41.

27 P. Cawson, *Young Offenders in Care*, London: DHSS, 1980.

28 See S. Millham, R. Bullock and K. Hosie, *Locking Up Children: Secure Provision within the Child Care System*, London: Saxon House, 1978.

Chapter Three

INTERMEDIATE TREATMENT

The 1968 White Paper *Children in Trouble* put forward the idea of intermediate treatment, a kind of half-way stage between removing young offenders from their parents' home and working with them solely at home.

The theory of intermediate treatment (IT) appears to have been based on the idea that much juvenile offending is stimulated by the offenders' participation in a 'delinquent subculture'. This notion has been accepted for a long time, although its definition has undergone a considerable evolution. Albert Cohen[1] expressed the view that this group or subculture was made up of lower-class youths whose delinquency represented an opposition to the prevalent middle-class culture and norms, and that in turn this behaviour became their norm, the requirement for belonging to this alternative culture. Others expanded and developed the thesis and in 1960 Cloward and Ohlin[2] formalized this subculture by considering that it had its own values and norms which were so strong that those who contravened them would be expelled from the group. This was questioned by Matza,[3] who proposed that young people's commitment to delinquency could be a pretence undertaken to gain the acceptance of their peers, and thus that delinquent behaviour by groups resulted from a process of mutual (if unwitting) deception, as well as from conscious choice. When the natural disintegration of the group occurred because its members went their separate ways to marry, to be educated, or to do their military service, the delinquency ceased. 'The drift' (Matza's term) had been halted.

If delinquent behaviour depends so heavily on peer involvement and approval, one solution to it would be to weaken attachment to the peer-group at an early stage and to substitute attachment to other cultural norms instead. It is not recorded that the authors of the White Paper followed precisely this argument, but it seems likely that their thinking ran along similar lines.

The idea of intermediate treatment was taken into the 1969 Children and Young Persons Act and, although the term itself does not appear in the legislation, it is used in the guide to the Act, where it describes the requirements which may be included in a supervision order (Sections 12 and 18 of the Act). Within the Department of Health and Social Security, the Intermediate Treatment Development Group set up a number of pilot schemes and published two guidance booklets as well as providing a grant for an information service operated by the National Youth Bureau. Nevertheless, it was some time before anything which would be termed intermediate treatment began to operate as such. Although the Act became law on 1 January, 1971, the first scheme was not introduced until July 1973. In part this delay can be explained by the organizational problems of setting up and co-ordinating such schemes. While local authority social services departments had the power to set up schemes, the responsibility for planning and co-ordinating them, and for integrating voluntary and local government initiatives, rested with the twelve Children's Regional Planning Committees (who had a similar task with respect to the provision of community homes). The first Regional Plans were produced in 1973 and it was only with this event that intermediate treatment can be said to have been launched.

There was, however, and still is, the problem of identifying what intermediate treatment was. In some areas 'ready-made' schemes were already available; in others, newly appointed Intermediate Treatment Officers, given the responsibility for the new provision, had hurriedly to invent or discover new facilities.

There is little doubt that the arrival of intermediate treatment caused a considerable amount of confusion. Part of this confusion arose from the fact that although it was a new term it did not involve a totally new method of intervention. Existing social work methods and facilities were to be used alongside the development of additional resources. While in theory it may be important to make a clear distinction between intermediate treatment, which is a legal concept, a requirement attached to an order of a court, and 'ordinary' social work with juveniles, in practice they may well be the same thing.

The phrase 'intermediate *treatment*' seems to support the 'medical model' of delinquency – the idea that selected treatment of offenders (treatment usually based on models of psychotherapy) can cure them and return them to normal, non-offending, behaviour. We have already suggested that the original proposers of intermediate treatment were influenced by what might be described as an 'infection model' of delinquency – the ideas of peer-group persuasion elucidated by Cohen and Matza and others – and certainly many of the projects used as intermediate treatment are designed to provide activities in which young people can feel a sense of achievement and can gain or restore their self-confidence.[4] Other projects have attempted to be remedial – to compensate, as it were, for what are seen as delinquency-producing environments, not only at home but also in the community or at school.[5]

Thus intermediate treatment has come to encompass a multiplicity of forms of intervention. In part this is a development to be welcomed. Alternatives to custody can hope to succeed, it seems to us, only if they address themselves, in part at least, to the reasons why people offend and are convicted by the courts. As non-custodial sentences are by their nature generally less punitive than custodial ones,[6] they should demonstrate among their subjects some measure of rehabilitation or diversion from further offending (whether over a long or short period) or from the worst effects of the criminal justice system. To achieve these aims the sentence should be structured according to a theory of delinquency. The various 'pathological' theories of delinquency that once held sway, and produced the 'treatment' idea, are no longer unchallenged – as we have seen – but they have not been succeeded by any one theory.

In a situation, therefore, where we recognize a plurality of theories 'explaining' delinquency and identifying the causes of its beginning or perpetuation, it is perhaps not unreasonable that there should be, within the framework of one sentence, a plurality of approaches to deal with juvenile offending. (It also seems reasonable that those different approaches should be evaluated to see how far they succeed, and on what terms. The observation of practice should be used to test the theories on which practice is based.) At the same time, the diversity of approaches to intermediate treatment may have tended to weaken its impact. Thus the DHSS Intermediate Treatment Development Group, attempting a definition, could only offer the points that it was intended as a court disposal, 'intermediate' between custody or care and parental control, exercised at the discretion of the supervisor, intended to benefit the juvenile, and using facilities that may be used by children not subject to supervision orders.[7]

This does not give much positive guidance on what was envisaged, and neither did the Act itself, so it was left to the Children's Regional Planning Committees to determine local provision. This provision has been uneven, however. An article on the subject, in *Justice of the Peace* (9 January, 1982), suggested that proper IT schemes providing alternatives to custody were operational only in about half of England and Wales.[8] What provision there is has been manifestly unable to halt the juvenile courts' increasing use of custodial sentences. In 1978 only 12 per cent of the 33,000 current supervision orders contained a requirement of intermediate treatment. (About 7,000 juveniles were sentenced to borstal or detention centre that year.)

While under-resourcing may be one reason for intermediate

treatment's apparent lack of impact as a non-custodial alternative, another cause may be sought in the expansion of many schemes to take in not only offenders but also, as a preventative measure, children 'at risk'. Such diversionary projects can certainly be justified if they can be demonstrated to be effective, but there is the danger that the diversion they achieve is not from custody.

From the beginning of intermediate treatment there were a wide variety of interpretations of its nature and of the needs it was intended to serve. In part this was a result of the philosophy behind the Children and Young Persons Act 1969: that there were no or few essential differences between deprived and delinquent young people. Thus the courts were given the ability to impose conditions in supervision orders whose length they could control but whose nature and purpose were to be determined by the social workers (or probation officers) administering them. This, together with the rather looser framework for intervention given by supervision orders as compared with probation orders, meant that the courts, as the framers of the Act doubtless intended, appeared to be giving some of their discretion in sentencing over to social work professionals, who would devise a programme of work (treatment) to ensure that the young delinquent did not come back to court.

Inevitably perhaps, many, if not most, of the first IT schemes were based on existing resources provided by local Youth Services and voluntary agencies. At least one of these agencies saw IT as a preventative measure aimed at young people on the threshold of a criminal career, rather than at more disturbed or difficult offenders, and foresaw, not unnaturally, problems of fitting delinquents into its normal framework of activities.[9] In addition to these problems of assimilation, there arose related difficulties of fitting together social workers' responsibilities for supervising court orders with the kind of worker–client relationships that were the norm for these early programmes – based as they were principally on leisure and adventure activities.[10] It is fair to say that difficulties in reconciling the perspectives of workers who have individual responsibilities for their clients with those of the projects to which those clients have been referred remain a constant problem of social work practice.

The difficulties that have been alluded to above appear to have helped to prompt many local authorities to develop their own 'in-house' IT facilities, staffed from within their social services departments. It is probable that this only speeded up an inevitable development, as authorities wished to have more control over the facilities available to them.[11] The general model of IT development by social services departments was to appoint one or more IT officers – based either centrally or in district or area offices, depending on the size of the department and the resources available – to develop and co-ordinate provision. The work of these officers became increasingly that of setting up 'in-house' projects – for instance, the establishment of 'IT centres' or more simple group (and/or activity) programmes. These developments, however, did not necessarily clarify the nature of IT.

The Children and Young Persons' Act had allowed for two kinds of IT conditions: an intensive ninety-day period of 'treatment' (including the possibility of a residential placement), and a condition of attending an IT scheme for up to thirty (separate) days a year. Thus a distinction could be made between 'intensive' and 'ordinary' IT (although this was abolished by the Criminal Law Act of 1977, which provided for all IT conditions to be of up to ninety days). Local authority social services departments were also the heirs of children's departments, which had already been given powers, under Section 1 of the Children and Young Persons Act 1963, to act to prevent children being taken into care. It could be argued that the 1969 Act in effect extended this kind of preventative function to children at risk of coming before the courts,[12] and these considerations perhaps affected the wide spectrum of approaches to IT.

At one end of the spectrum, once known colloquially as 'the heavy end', lies the idea of IT as a sentence of the court, fitting into the tariff between custody or care and a supervision order. From this perspective the purpose of IT is to offer an alternative to a custodial or institutional court order; the intention is that the application of appropriate forms of 'treatment' will divert subjects from further offending. Generally the kind of 'treatment' used is 'intensive', based loosely on the ninety-day model, although often with less emphasis on residential placements and more on attending an IT centre. Some commentators note that IT is a scarce resource, and should therefore be used primarily for those most in need of immediate diversion from threatened custodial sentences or institutional placements. The justification for schemes based on this model rests, therefore, on their ability to affect court orders and to reform offenders referred to them.[13]

At the other end of the spectrum are concepts of IT as early intervention to prevent, divert, contain or inhibit behaviour that might later bring children into contact with the courts, and therefore put them at risk of custody or care. In this kind of model IT is seen as an attempt to remedy or alleviate special kinds of deprivation suffered by children 'at risk', whether these are engendered by individual, family or environmental factors or caused by, for example, the interaction between children and the schools they attend (or did attend before they were barred from them).[14] While much work within this 'at risk' model is again very intensive, little, if any, is done within the structure of a supervision order, and indeed the very existence of one might be regarded as denoting the failure of such a project.

Finally, the middle points of the spectrum appear to be filled with IT schemes, perhaps the majority, that attempt to combine some form of 'early prevention' with the supervision of some delinquents on IT conditions. Generally, these schemes, perhaps because they fall between the extremes of pure prevention and pure court disposal, seem less intense than the 'infra-reds' and 'ultra-violets' of the spectrum. But they are also most at risk of falling prey to confusion and conflict between IT as prevention and IT as 'cure', which can lead to the kind of pathetic mismatch between grandiose project aims (to change all adverse aspects of a juvenile's life and behaviour) and simple methods of intervention (two weekends' pony-trekking) criticized by Jones and Kerslake.[15]

While the differences in purpose between IT projects can thus be vast, there is perhaps more common ground between them in terms of their operational philosophies and policies. Firstly, most if not all IT projects rest on the concept of providing resources to meet children's *needs* – although they may differ about how they perceive and define these needs. Secondly, most IT projects are based on the idea of group work;[16] and thirdly, these groups have tended to focus either on leisure-type activities or on 'social skills'. (Indeed, the relative lack of concentration of IT on educational problems (with exceptions)[17] and on providing employment for young people likely to be permanently jobless, has been criticized by Trevor Locke.)[18] Fourthly, IT projects are reported to see diversion of their clients from (further) offending, and, if necessary, from custodial or institutional orders by the courts, as central to their functioning.

In part, the variety of schemes going under the title of IT may have been increased by the DHSS's views on its role. For example, the 1976 White Paper[19] responding to the Eleventh Report of the House of Commons Expenditure Committee on the working of the Children and Young Persons Act 1969, emphasized the preventative role of IT. This may be regarded as a widening of IT beyond the type of resource apparently allowed by the Act, and may be seen as part of a contemporary emphasis on providing non-institutional care in the social services.[20] Since then the provisions of the Criminal Justice Act 1982 have shifted IT back to being a sentence of the court. Specifically, this Act gives courts the power to make conditions in supervision orders restricting the behaviour of juveniles – in particular to impose a temporary 'curfew' on them – and to require juveniles to attend stipulated 'activity' schemes run by the supervising agency. Also, the responsibility for planning IT provision has been taken away from Regional Planning Committees and handed to social services departments in conjunction with their local probation services (which are supposed to approve any plans). This appears to be accompanied by a growing willingness of the Government to allow funding for IT schemes, or their analogues, run by the probation service.

Theoretical arguments apart, local authorities have had good practical reasons for not emphasizing IT as an alternative to custody. Like community homes and assessment centres but unlike borstals and detention centres (now youth custody and detention centres), IT has been financed by local authorities and planned (until 1983) by their representatives on Regional Planning Committees.

This division of responsibility was not envisaged in the Children and Young Persons Act 1969, which provided for the replacement of detention centres by community homes, and for the restriction of borstal sentences to offenders aged 17 to 20. It is here that the partial implementation of the Act is most to be regretted as it has failed to give local authorities any short-term financial interest in reducing the population of custodial institutions; by promoting IT as an alternative to custody, social services departments are taking on extra responsibilities, which require more resources, without receiving any direct benefit. By contrast, IT projects can be cheaper than expensive placements in community homes, and so departments may see some benefit to their estimates, as well as to their clients, by promoting IT in this area. Thus, when social services departments are devoted ideologically to using IT as an alternative to custody, this may become difficult for the local authority to justify in terms of 'value for money'.

The preceding argument may appear cynical, and it is *not* intended to impugn the motives of social workers who refer to IT projects, nor those of the IT workers themselves, but only to suggest that it is hardly surprising that local authorities, in a decade of financial restraint (to say the least), should have declined to emphasize the non-custodial aspects of IT. Indeed, an unexpectedly high proportion, against their apparent short-term financial self-interest, have espoused a policy of using IT specifically as an alternative sentence.

The other side of the issue of whether and how far IT should be fixed at this end of the spectrum is a question about how in general social workers can work most effectively with young people to reduce their offending. Should this be by intervening only after an offence (serious enough to warrant a custodial sentence) has been committed, or by providing services aimed at deprived and disturbed young people who may be particularly likely to offend? (It should be noted that this only becomes an issue framed in these terms because of the perceived inadequacies of the pathological model of offending and its treatment. If that model were believed to be true, IT could be discussed in terms of whether or not it represented an appropriate response to the 'symptoms' presented to the court.)

Linked to this are questions about the appropriateness of other forms of social work with juveniles, as well as the question of whether young delinquents are different from the generality of deprived young people. Jones and Kerslake[21] criticize social workers for resorting too early to care orders for juveniles – a criticism that seems to be echoed in one IT centre's view of itself as taking children other people were apparently unable to work with.[22] Similarly a practice in one department of using social worker resources relatively more for supervising stable long-term placements of children in care and thus meeting statutory responsibilities while giving over a significant proportion of more difficult and demanding work with 'problem families' to relatively untrained and inexperienced auxiliary workers was noted in one research study.[23]

These problems may be partly due to poor planning and inappropriate policies, but perhaps they also show that 'difficult and disturbed' children represent a problem for social services and education departments *before* they ever get to court, and this in turn may justify both the idea of IT as prevention, and the dominance of working with groups of young people as the preferred method of intervention.

A study, referred to above, of the caseload of an area office in one local authority social services department, gives an insight into the position of juvenile delinquency among the multiplicity of problems facing such an agency. In the office studied, children's cases – children in care, cases of family problems involving children, and overt cases of juvenile delinquency – made up about a third of the office's allocated caseload; fewer than one in ten of these cases was described as 'juvenile delinquency' (3 per cent of the total caseload), but a significant proportion of the children in the two-thirds of children's cases described as 'problems of child behaviour and family relationships' had a past history of court orders and institutional placements, suggesting delinquent behaviour in the past.

In the context of our present discussion it is important to note some other salient features of these cases. Firstly, they were described as presenting 'chronic and severe' problems both in terms of the way family members behaved and in terms of the deprivation they suffered; secondly, these cases consumed a considerable amount of social work resources with very little sign that they could be helped effectively by the kind of service the department (or any department) could give; and thirdly, it followed that the work in these cases could hardly be described as 'preventative' in the sense of taking early action to alleviate severe later problems. Rather these cases seem to epitomize the failure of prior attempts (most of the children central to the cases were in their late teens) at 'prevention'.[24]

The picture that emerges from this study, as from the Cambridge Delinquency Study (albeit with a different emphasis),[25] is of juvenile delinquency as the tip of an iceberg of deprivation and distress, and while it may be argued that confirmed delinquents present specific problems requiring special resources there seems little doubt that the needs of deprived families in general are just as great.

From this standpoint then, IT can be regarded as a way of working with children and young people for whom the normal resources of social work are insufficient because of the severity and complexity of their problems and needs. For them, IT centres can be a resource when everyone else, including school, seems unable to deal with them. It appears, however, that it is principally the availability of such centres, and their capacity to accept and keep children that virtually every other community agency has rejected, that is important, rather than their commitment to specific styles of social work intervention. For example, a report on IT work in Wandsworth stresses that it was the range and flexibility of resources, programmes and services – including counselling, information provision, group work and family work – offered by IT centres that enabled them to keep and help in the community the children and young people referred to them.[26]

Such wide eclecticism and such a variety of resources may still be uncommon in IT, but this report does stress, as do other writers,[27] that IT is not a specific and defined entity, but rather a portmanteau into which a set of alternatives to 'traditional' casework can be packed. Of these the most common is group work,[28] which has been seen as particularly appropriate for young people because many of the theories of why they offend (and present problems to 'authority' in other ways) stress the role of peer-groups. Other children may be labelled as 'disruptive' or 'backward', for example, because of the way they behave in the group situation of school.[29] In addition, as adolescence is a time of stress for which the surest cure seems to be 'growing up', more reflective styles of intervention may in any case have limited value. Thus, while group work may not be the right approach for all those referred to IT, it seems to be the preferred method for most. The groups themselves can vary considerably in content, structure and objectives. Many of the early IT schemes relied on 'Outward Bound'-type 'adventure' activities – mountaineering, canoeing, sailing, etc. – as the main form of group work. More recently the emphasis seems to have shifted towards groups focused on practical problems and social skills, but it seems probable that in most settings it is the experience and functioning of the group that is important, rather than its devotion to highly specific objects (although these may emerge and be worked on at various times during a group's life).

In this, however, there is a danger. One of the reasons advanced for the apparent ineffectiveness of 'residential treatment' in 'curing' delinquency was that skills learned in coping with the therapeutic regime of a hostel or home might not be useful or used in the world outside.[30] Similarly, as not all human interaction takes place in groups, it might be argued that too great a concentration on group work will leave its recipients able only to function in 'group-work' (as opposed to group) situations. In practice, however, this danger seems remote; in many if not most 'middle-range' IT projects the intensity of the work done with young people is probably relatively low (one or two group sessions a week). Furthermore, commentators stress the importance of structuring groups to 'wean' participants from potential dependency.[31] Nevertheless, given the apparent centrality of group-work concepts to IT, it seems important that emphasis is given to evaluating the methods used, and their effects, as well as to studying the general outcomes (in terms, for example, of conviction rates) of the projects themselves.[32]

The report on IT in Wandsworth saw the work as being primarily 'preventative' (of crime) and cited evidence to oppose the contention that preventative IT was ineffective and indeed often counter-productive in that its 'failures' appeared to receive harsher sentences from the courts. The contributors argued that the intensity of their provision was an important factor in their success not only in keeping their clients out of the courts, but also in apparently persuading magistrates to deal relatively leniently with them if they did offend.[33] Comparisons between different courts' sentencing policies are difficult to interpret, however, and it is perhaps more productive to consider instead the nature of 'preventative' IT.

We have already observed that, in one social services department's caseload, the problems presented by the situations of children who are being maintained in the community can be so severe and complex that 'attempted containment' might be a better term than 'prevention' to describe social workers' attempts to deal with them. There seem to be no reasons to believe that the evidence presented above for this situation is very atypical in the range of problems presented, nor in the fact that juvenile delinquency was apparently the major problem in only a minority of cases. It follows, therefore, that, as we have said, most of the work of social services departments with children and their families will follow the failure of any preventative measures that may have been adopted earlier, and that this work will *not* usually focus on delinquency (although it may be concerned with factors associated with offending).[34] In such attempts at containment – at preventing children's perceived behaviour escalating to (further) offending – it seems to us that intensive provision has an important role to perform, as it may well be better suited to the tasks at hand than is conventional social work practice. Whether IT is then an appropriate description for such a function may be, and has been, queried.[35]

On the other hand, it may be argued that such intensive provision is the least that should be made available to meet these needs. If this is so – and the proposition has not, so far as we know, been tested – then the 'middle range' provision of less intensive intervention, especially with 'low risk' children, may be less easy to justify, except in so far as it diverts young offenders from institutional placements or sentences. Here it should be noted that 'diversion programs' in America (aimed at diverting juveniles entirely from court proceedings) have been criticized for concentrating on those who were unlikely to offend (again) in any case, or who were unlikely to go into custody for their current offence, leaving 'high risk' young offenders to be processed by the courts and to receive the custodial sentences these programmes were designed to reduce.[36]

In this field, 'intensive' IT thus remains the only specific alternative to custody. Because, it seems, of the DHSS's early emphasis on prevention, and because of the ways the schemes developed, this has often been underemphasized. Nevertheless it seems to us that to provide an alternative to custody is the only justification for including an IT requirement in a supervision order (as opposed to referring a juvenile to what may be called an IT project). If this is so then it should follow that the work done by such compulsory IT schemes should reflect and should attempt to deal with their clients' offending behaviour – or those elements in it that prompted the court to consider custody. Thus the role of IT as a non-custodial alternative should prompt the sponsors and resourcers of such schemes to think clearly about their intended objectives, and how these will be met by each scheme. We would also argue that more distinction should be made between this form of IT and the so-called 'preventative' projects, whose function of keeping juveniles out of court, while equally, if not more important, seems to be significantly different.

Has intermediate treatment failed? We have seen that its introduction has had no perceptible effect on courts' propensity to imprison offenders. Similarly the success of intermediate treatment considered only as a style or mode of social work intervention has not on the whole been startling.

The Government's response has been, in effect, to 'beef up' intermediate treatment by introducing in the 1982 Criminal Justice Act 'supervised activity orders', allowing the courts to require offenders to take part in specified programmes, and involving the probation service more in this kind of provision. In some ways, this development, recognizing the particular nature of IT as a non-custodial measure, might be welcomed, *if* the resources were made available for appropriate schemes as well as for intensive 'preventative' provision. It may be, however, that the results will be counterproductive. The present problems of intermediate treatment are also in some senses virtues. We know very little about what kinds of intervention are, by any standards, effective as realistic alternatives to custody for juveniles. In this situation, the eclecticism of intermediate treatment schemes can, properly used, be a strength. As we have seen, while there is evidence, in West and Farrington's study of South London boys,[37] that juveniles who repeatedly offend differ in certain respects from the majority of their peers (who would themselves be considered 'deviant' by adult, middle-class standards), the same study suggests that the distinctions between offenders and non-offenders are hard to predict and may not justify different forms of intervention. It is probable, therefore, that treating young people differently on the basis only of whether they have been found guilty of an offence may perpetuate the problem, not solve it. Unless and until we know more about the appropriateness of different types of provision we must also remember that some intermediate treatment schemes do appear to be successful as alternatives to custody.

Keep Out, an organization launched in December 1981 to reduce the use of custody for young people, points to a scheme run by Essex social services department which has apparently succeeded in reducing the total number of custodial sentences and residential care placements for juveniles by 25 per cent over a three-year period, halving the number sent to borstal,[38] and allowing the department to close one of its local community homes with education (formerly known as approved schools).

In addition to such reported successes, intermediate treatment has the value that, as it has developed, it presents an alternative approach to the more regulatory non-custodial sentences available for juveniles. As we have seen, intensive preventative provision may hold the seeds of a wider movement to divert juveniles from the attentions of the criminal justice system, and such positive diversion seems badly needed. West and Farrington's study demonstrates the relative failure of traditional treatment-oriented methods, both custodial and non-custodial, of sentencing juveniles (and the failure of 'punishment').

Similarly, a recent report on the results of the Wakefield IT project, operating specifically as an alternative to incarceration and attempting to change offending behaviour, shows encouraging results by comparison with placements in community homes with education, which are themselves the first stage of custodial sentencing.[39]

As Robert Adams[40] points out in a thought-provoking conclusion to a review of four intermediate treatment schemes, the apparently radical approaches of total decarceration of young offenders as in Massachusetts[41] or of the acclimatization of society to tolerate juvenile delinquency through a policy of benign neglect do not seem credible or likely solutions.

While not totally accepting Adams' critique of the juvenile justice system as a form of class repression of the young, we do see the system as it stands, and as it has recently been 'reformed', as counter-productive. The 1969 Act, as implemented and operated, has led to more juveniles being sent into custody, and it is apparent that a different approach is needed.

Although intermediate treatment schemes have not always been well evaluated, there is evidence that some of them can divert offenders from custody and young people from being sentenced by the courts. The juvenile panel system in Scotland also shows that it is possible to deal with delinquents informally, and to cut down the number of custodial sentences imposed without promoting a juvenile crime wave. It may be that in England and Wales intermediate treatment is the first step in providing better alternatives for young people.

NOTES AND REFERENCES

1 A. Cohen, *Delinquent Boys: The Culture of the Gang*, London: Collier-Macmillan, 1955.

2 R.A. Cloward and L.E. Ohlin, *Delinquency and Opportunity*, London: Routledge & Kegan Paul, 1960.

3 D. Matza, *Becoming Deviant*, New Jersey: Prentice-Hall, 1969.

4 On a link between self-esteem and delinquency see, for example, M. Norris, 'Use of Repertory Grid in Investigating Change in Trainees at a Detention Centre', *British Journal of Criminology*, Vol. 17, No. 3, 1977, pp. 274–9. The relationship between self-concept and delinquency was tested by W. Reckless and S. Dinitz, 'Self Concept and Delinquency', *The Journal of Criminal Law*, Vol. 58, 1967, pp. 519–23.

5 See, for example, D. Reynolds and D. Jones, 'Education and the Prevention of Juvenile Delinquency', in N. Tutt (ed.), *Alternative Strategies for Coping with Crime*, London: Basil Blackwell and Martin Rochester, 1978.

6 Although some critics of treatment have regarded long probation orders as being more severe than short custodial sentences, we would not agree with them. See Chapter 4.

7 DHSS Development Group, *Intermediate Treatment*, London: DHSS, 1977.

8 'Brougham', 'Probation v. Intermediate Treatment', *Justice of the Peace*, Vol. 146, No. 2, 1982, p. 29.

9 M.F. Bacon, *Intermediate Treatment Involvement*, London: National Association of Boys' Clubs, 1973.

10 R. Jones and A. Kerslake, *Intermediate Treatment and Social Work*, London: Heinemann Educational, 1979.

11 Ibid.

12 See Personal Social Services Council, *A Future for Intermediate Treatment: Report of the Intermediate Treatment Study Group*, London: PSSC, 1977.

13 See, for example, P. Stougler, 'IT at the Heavy End of Delinquency', *Community Care*, No. 353, 1981, pp. 14–15, and D. Thorpe, 'Diverting Delinquents', *Community Care*, No. 366, 1981, p. 21.

14 See E. Leggett (ed.), *Wandsworth: A Multi-Disciplinary Approach to Intermediate Treatment*, London: National Youth Bureau, 1979.

15 R. Jones and A. Kerslake, *Intermediate Treatment and Social Work*, op. cit., p. 10.

16 Ibid. and E. Leggett (ed.), *Wandsworth*, op. cit.

17 See E. Leggett (ed.), *Wandsworth*, op. cit.

18 T. Locke, *Planning: Strategic and Practical Options in Work with Young People in Trouble*, London: Intermediate Treatment Resource Centre Ideas Exchange, 1982.

19 Home Office, Welsh Office, DHSS and DES, *Children and Young Persons Act 1969: Observations on the Eleventh Report from the Expenditure Committee*, London: HMSO, 1976.

20 See Personal Social Services Council, *A Future for Intermediate Treatment*, op. cit.

21 R. Jones and A. Kerslake, *Intermediate Treatment and Social Work*, op. cit., pp. 99–100.

22 E. Leggett (ed.), *Wandsworth*, op. cit.

23 E.M. Goldberg and R.W. Warburton, *Ends and Means in Social Work*, London: Allen & Unwin, 1979.

24 Ibid., pp. 103–8.

25 See D.J. West, *Delinquency: Its Roots, Careers and Prospects*, London: Heinemann, 1982; D.J. West and D.P. Farrington, *Who Becomes Delinquent?*, London: Heinemann, 1973, and *The Delinquent Way of Life*, London: Heinemann, 1977.

26 E. Leggett (ed.), *Wandsworth*, op. cit.

27 R. Jones and A. Kerslake, *Intermediate Treatment and Social Work*, op.cit.

28 In Wandsworth, for example, the most common forms of IT were small groups and clubs – involving up to half of those referred. See E. Leggett (ed.), *Wandsworth*, op. cit., p. 13.

29 For example, West and Farrington's work (see note 25) suggests that many subsequent delinquents were not well thought of by their teachers.

30 D.B. Cornish and R.V.G. Clarke, *Residential Treatment and Its Effects on Delinquency*, Home Office Research Study No. 32, London: HMSO, 1975.

31 See E. Leggett (ed.), *Wandsworth*, op. cit., and R. Jones and A. Kerslake, *Intermediate Treatment and Social Work*, op. cit.

32 See J. Downie and J. Ames, *Intermediate Treatment Research*, University of Sheffield Joint Unit for Social Services Research in collaboration with *Community Care*, 1981, for a discussion of possible approaches to evaluating IT in Scotland.

33 E. Leggett (ed.), *Wandsworth*, op. cit., pp. 34 and 35.

34 See D.J. West and D.P. Farrington, *Who Becomes Delinquent?* and *The Delinquent Way of Life*, op. cit.

35 E. Leggett (ed.), *Wandsworth*, op. cit.

36 M.W. Klein, 'Deinstitutionalization and Diversion of Juvenile Offenders', in N. Morris and M. Tonry (eds), *Crime and Justice*, Vol. 1, Chicago and London: University of Chicago Press, 1979, pp. 145–201.

37 D.J. West and D.P. Farrington, *The Delinquent Way of Life*, op. cit.

38 *Keep Out Spotlight on Essex*, London: Keep Out, 1982.

39 J. Denne and R. Peel, 'Does IT Work?', *Community Care*, No. 454, 1983, pp. 20 and 21.

40 R. Adams, S. Allard, J. Baldwin and J. Thomas, *A Measure of Diversion? Case Studies in Intermediate Treatment*, London: National Youth Bureau Publications, 1981.

41 See Chapter 8 for a fuller discussion of this development.

Chapter Four

THE COURSE OF THE PROBATION ORDER

A quarter of a century ago, when it had been available to the courts as an alternative to custody for over fifty years, probation, described by Sir Leon Radzinowicz as 'a form of social service preventing further crime by readjustment of the culprit',[1] seemed to be, in Bottoms and McWilliams' phrase, 'the jewel in the crown of the "new penology"'.[2] About one person in five guilty of an indictable offence received a probation order,[3] and probation, which in the eyes of one influential observer seemed destined to outlast all other ways of sentencing offenders,[4] was about to enter a brief golden age.

Some twenty or more years later, the court disposal that had been viewed as the keystone of the Government's penal policy appeared to be in danger of being rejected by the builders of contemporary strategies of dealing with offenders. By 1981, only 7 per cent of persons sentenced for an indictable offence received a probation order – and a further 3 per cent a supervision order.[5] Thus, in two decades, probation (and its successor in the juvenile courts – supervision) was used by the courts only about half as often, in relation to the number of offenders found guilty, as it had been in 1960. In fact, over this period, the decline in the courts' use of supervision and probation for juveniles, young persons and adults appears to have been of about the same order of magnitude for each of these groups.[6] Since 1980 the probation order at least seems to have been holding its position, and its use has increased in proportion to the rise in the number of cases coming before the courts. Nevertheless, over the last twenty-five years as a whole, the place of the probation order in the pattern of sentences used by the courts and its role as *the* alternative to custody do seem to have changed.

It is not our purpose to investigate in detail the reasons for this change, although some will become apparent to the reader, but rather to consider some of the current arguments surrounding the probation order and their implications for its future as a non-custodial sentence. To understand the issues, however, we must first outline the history and development of probation itself.

While some English magistrates had experimented during the nineteenth century with various devices, such as the use of 'magistrates' bail', to suspend sentence in order to keep individuals out of prison and yet responsible to the court for their future good behaviour, the concept of probation itself was first developed in the American state of Massachusetts in the middle years of that century (Massachusetts had a recognizable, court-based probation system by 1869). After several false starts, the pattern of this first 'Massachusetts experiment' was adapted for England in the 1907 Probation of Offenders Act.

Dorothy Bochel, in her history of the probation service,[7] argues that the introduction of probation to this country was due primarily to pressure from reformist individuals and bodies such as the Howard Association, and to their promoting the merits of the Massachusetts system. Earlier or contemporary English experiments such as 'magistrates' bail' and the work of the police court missionaries were, she argues, unconnected with or, at best, tangential to this development, although they had a common root in desires to lessen the courts' use of imprisonment.

Nevertheless, when the time came to appoint probation officers under the new Act, most courts which had the opportunity to do so appointed the police court missionary attached to the court and these appointments may be said to have helped to set the tone of the probation service as a caring agency, rather than one dedicated solely to the enforcement of the law.[8] Thus the Inner London Probation Service, for example, clearly sees the police court missionaries as the forerunners of present-day probation officers, and in 1976 celebrated the centenary of the appointment of the first of the missionaries – to Bow Street police court – as the beginning of the probation service.[9]

The police court missionaries were appointed not as agents of the court but to work for the Church of England Temperance Society to 'rescue' offenders, and particularly to persuade them to 'take the pledge' and give up drinking in order to break the cycle of crime and imprisonment. Inevitably their work went beyond this somewhat fundamentalist aim to provide a form of general social work service for the courts, and through this they became involved, at the magistrates' behest, in the 'supervision' of offenders. At first the opportunities for this were limited, but they grew with the passing of the First Offenders Act in 1887, which allowed magistrates to release first offenders on their own recognizance with the opportunity to demonstrate contrition or reform before they returned to court for sentence. Although the missionaries had no formal status under this

Act, they were often used by magistrates to supervise and help first offenders. Thus, before the 1907 Probation of Offenders Act, police court missionaries were already carrying out many tasks analogous to those of later probation officers.

It should not be forgotten either that ideas of the possible rehabilitation and treatment of offenders through 'social work' were, at this time, gaining greater currency among reformers and in the Home Office.

The early years of probation were to encapsulate many of the issues and problems that have since bedevilled the probation service. The place of probation as an alternative to custody, the selection of clients for probation and the low use of probation by courts were all matters of concern in the first decade of the service, and remain central to our discussion of it today. Thus, before the 1907 Act was implemented, the Chairman of the Prison Commissioners, Sir Evelyn Ruggles-Brise (who was one of the foremost advocates of a regulatory function for probation), wrote to the Home Secretary:

> . . . 'probation' in the real sense is a State scheme for furnishing an alternative to commitment to prison, with all that that implies, of that vast multitude of offenders who commit trivial and unimportant offences. . . .[10]

Ruggles-Brise had supported the idea of a probation order because of the hope it offered of reducing an excessive prison population, and he was afraid that what he called 'philanthropists' were bent on orientating it towards child offenders who were at this time rarely imprisoned by comparison with adults. His concern was that by doing so they would render probation less effective as an alternative to custody. As we shall see, this is not a dead issue even three-quarters of a century later.

Soon after the Act was implemented, the question of the kind of person for whom probation was appropriate also arose. As Miss Lucy Bartlett, a leading member of the Penal Reform League, told the Home Secretary, 'The right choice of cases in the first place [by the magistrate] is as important an element in probation as the right supervision of them afterwards.'[11] The issue behind this comment was that magistrates used the new probation order much less than had been hoped. In 1908 probation orders were made only in about 11 per cent of cases brought before summary courts for indictable offences.[12] The Home Office, feeling that this proportion was too small (the equivalent figure in 1980 was also 11 per cent – 7 per cent probation orders and 4 per cent supervision orders for juveniles), was enquiring into the reasons for the low take-up of the new disposal by magistrates, and Lucy Bartlett was suggesting that magistrates needed guidance to select the right kind of cases for it. Some five years later this kind of argument had already taken the form of advocating the need for assessment before treatment.[13] The League for Penal Reform, for example, urged that a probation officer should make a (social) investigation prior to sentencing in every juvenile court case. (This proposal was not adopted in law until the 1947 Criminal Justice Act.)

It is probable that these issues, which cluster around the questions of 'who should be on probation, and why?', arise naturally, as it were, from the nature of the probation order. In law probation is not a sentence in the same way as is imprisonment or a fine, even though the 1982 Criminal Justice Act allowed offenders to appeal against probation orders as they already could against fines or prison sentences. It is instead an opportunity for offenders to demonstrate their ability for reform, while being allowed to live in the community and not being subject to any other penalty. A probation order is made for a fixed period (currently of any length between six months and three years), and if an offender successfully completes that period he or she cannot be sentenced in any other way for the original offence. A probation order may be terminated and replaced by another sentence if the offender (client) is in breach of its conditions, or if he or she reoffends; the order may also be terminated early 'for good progress', or substituted by a conditional discharge if there seems no good reason to continue supervision by a probation officer; the length and conditions of the order can be varied on application by the client or supervising officer.

Perhaps the three key features of the probation order are that it can only be made with the consent of the offender, that it is intended to be to the offender's benefit, and that by making the order the court imposes certain conditions of behaviour upon the offender. Broadly speaking, these conditions, since the implementation of the 1982 Criminal Justice Act, are now of four kinds:

the standard conditions written into any probation order;

conditions which require an offender to submit to what might be described as 'treatment regimes' defined by statute – for example, to receive psychiatric treatment or to live in a probation hostel;

locally negotiated or imposed conditions requiring the offender to take part in a presumably helpful project or programme such as to take a course of driving lessons, to attend treatment for alcoholism, to participate in an employment project, or to attend a day centre;

local conditions directed at controlling an offender's behaviour: for example, to stay away from a football ground or to attend a day centre.

It is these conditions that are the greatest strength of the probation order but, at the same time, as the possibility of day centre attendance being both beneficial and controlling illustrates, provoke the most discussion and debate about its nature and value.

The strength of the probation order lies in the flexibility of its conditions and the way in which these can, in theory, be moulded to meet the client's needs. The weakness is that these conditions – defined originally as ways of regulating clients' lives and then as aids to treatment – now seem to present an uneasy mixture of coercion and intervention and can be interpreted not only as helpful interventions but also as unwarranted intrusions into clients' lives, as redundant formalities, or as anything else in between.

Before we plunge into the issues of this debate on 'care and control', it must be said that most, if not all, probation officers have learned to live with most of the apparent paradoxes of their situation and to achieve in their work a personal reconciliation of what others see as mutually irreconcilable aims and activities. This reconciliation has been achieved, however, principally through using what might be described as the informal conditions of probation; the encouragement that the Criminal Justice Act gives to formal encouragements or prohibitions of offenders' behaviour may make such adjustments more difficult to achieve.

The discussion, therefore, has been at one remove from probation officers' day-to-day practice. Nevertheless, it is important because of the context it gives both to recent developments in the courts' use of probation orders and also to consideration of the value of these orders as alternatives to prison.

The debate on care and control is rooted in the question of how the formal controls and conditions of a probation order interact with probation officers' exercise of their social work functions – including the injunction to 'advise, assist and befriend'. Entwined with this is the issue of whether the discretionary invocation of the formal conditions of probation is compatible with the just disposal of its clients.

One argument, exemplified by Phyllida Parsloe's paper to the 1978 Cropwood Conference,[14] is that the exercise of control over an offender is an integral part of the social work functions of a probation officer, in that the purpose of probation work is to guide the offender into making specific kinds of individual choices (against offending) in circumstances where he or she would not naturally have done so. This argument appears most cogent if we accept the assumptions of probation according to the treatment model – that delinquents are people who are identifiably different from non-delinquents, who act according to motives that are constrained by factors outside their control, and whose actions point to the need for intervention with respect to these factors.[15] The growing criticisms of this model in the last decade have tended to weaken this case, although, as Parsloe points out, probation officers' greater expertise and access to resources give a coercive aspect to any judgements that they may form of the interests of their clients.

Against this can be set the argument that while the basic legal conditions of the order, and the possibility of court proceedings for their breach, help to persuade the offender to conform to it, this only provides a framework for the working of the relationship between client and probation officer to bring about the changes necessary to help the client to avoid offending.[16] As Parsloe observes, the emphasis on voluntary change stemming from a voluntary decision to reform by the client leads on to the idea of separating the social work and controlling aspects of probation supervision.[17]

We should now, therefore, turn to attempts that have been made to separate the two aspects and the impact they appear to have had on probation practice. In 1978 a group of probation service managers (three Assistant Chief Probation Officers, a Deputy Chief and a Chief Probation Officer) published a paper entitled 'Sentenced to Social Work?'[18] in which they argued for a total separation between the formal conditions of the probation order and social work intervention. Briefly, their proposition was that the situation where the demands made on the client during supervision depended on his or her perceived response to the 'treatment' being offered was in fact a denial of justice, because the constraints so imposed on an offender bore no necessary relation to the offence, and were not an explicit part of the sentence. Thus, it was argued, someone put on probation for a less serious offence might lose more of his or her liberty than someone who had offended more seriously. It should therefore, they argued, be the responsibility of the court to set the conditions of the probation order, including the frequency with which the offender had to report to the probation service. The probation service in turn had a responsibility to offer help, advice and social work to the client, who was free to reject these offers without threat of further sanctions.

In addition to its arguments for linking 'justice' with help, 'Sentenced to Social Work?' contains a more subtle, but perhaps more telling, criticism of the mainstream of current probation practice in that in it the role of the probation officer as the supervisor of his or her clients is apparently questioned.

In the early days of the probation service each probation officer was personally responsible to the court that employed him or her for the offenders that he or she supervised. Reorganizations of the management and administration of the service (such as the introduction of Chief Probation Officers, Assistant Chief Probation Officers, etc.) and of the court system may have blurred this principle slightly, but it remains essentially true. True also, but less so as the service has acquired a variety of new resources and responsibilities, is the concept of the probation officer offering 'the complete and total service for which the agency exists',[19] in the sense that the kind of help a client receives from the service depends on what his or her supervising officer can provide.

The authors of 'Sentenced to Social Work?', however, suggest that the individual responsibility of a probation officer for supervising his or her clients should be commuted into a collective responsibility exercised through the person (not necessarily a probation officer) to whom the client reports and by the officers operating the varied services from which he or she can seek help.

The idea of the probation officer offering some form of assistance within the formal context of a requirement to report to him or her was also developed, from a more thoroughly argued theoretical base, by Bottoms and McWilliams in the 1979 paper 'A Non-Treatment Paradigm for Probation Practice'.[20] They argue firstly that the results of research have shown that treatment does not work, and secondly that the application of treatment is unjust because it coerces clients to receive it, and discounts or devalues their own views. Following these arguments, they propose the adoption of a model of intervention by probation officers with their clients based on 'help' rather than 'treatment'. This model they describe as follows:

> The caseworker . . . offers his unconditioned help with client-defined tasks, this offer having certain definite and defined boundaries. . . . If the offer is accepted, this leads to a collaborative effort between worker and client to define the problem requiring help, and to work out jointly a set of possible alternative strategies; the worker is also absolutely explicit about what kinds of help his agency can and cannot offer. The client is then left to make the choices for himself.[21]

In their paper, Bottoms and McWilliams draw clear distinctions not only between the enforcement of the basic reporting requirements of a probation order and the provision of 'help' to the client, but also between these two elements and the process by which probation officers, in writing 'social inquiry reports' (SIRs), inform the courts about offenders' backgrounds and advise about the appropriateness of certain sentences to the offender's personal circumstances.

The merits of this paradigm, they argue, are that it clearly places the authority for the control elements of probation (the formal conditions of the order) with the court, while the authority for the provision of help comes from the client, who requests it. Thus, the controlling power that in the treatment model (even in its weak form of 'social worker as expert') is linked with probation practice – indissolubly as Parsloe seems to argue – is explicitly detached from it, not only by separating off formal controls, but also by making the client the sole authority for any form of social work intervention. Similarly, Bottoms and McWilliams suggest that 'all recommendations [about sentencing] made by a probation officer in a social inquiry report must carry the consent of the client'.[22] They argue that this will tend to reduce the number of cases in which, following a recommendation in a social inquiry report, courts impose harsher sentences than justice demands.

Our concern with these proposals is not so much whether they represent good probation practice, although this is important, but whether they could enhance probation orders' ability to make a contribution to reducing the courts' use of custodial sentences. We must remember that the contributions to the 'care and control' debate that we have outlined here all accept that the twin functions of supervising offenders within the context of a court order and of providing some form of social work support must at least coexist within a probation order, and that it is this coexistence that gives probation its strength. At the same time, the decline during the 1970s in the courts' use of probation may in part be attributed to their dissatisfaction with probation practice, as interpreted to them. Is then the greater clarity about the formal conditions of probation argued for, in different ways, by 'Sentenced to Social Work?' and 'A Non-Treatment Paradigm for Probation Practice' likely to change sentencers' attitudes to probation?

As part of its programme of studying different approaches to directing offenders from custody within one English county (Hampshire), the Home Office Research Unit monitored the work of two probation teams using the 'Sentenced to Social Work?' approach of compulsory reporting at intervals set by the court alongside offers from the probation service of social work help. Preliminary findings, published in *Justice of the Peace*,[23] suggested that this new approach was less radical in its impact than might have been expected. The system of reporting seemed to achieve a slightly higher response rate than more 'traditional' approaches, although with no measurable impact on the rate at which clients reoffended during their orders. The rate at which clients took up offers of 'help' appeared to depend on the kind of help offered; more specific and structured assistance seemed to be used less often, perhaps because clients did not wish to identify personal problems that they saw as being related to their offending. Magistrates, however, were relatively unsympathetic to the ideas of 'justice' contained in this scheme, mainly because most of them professed more sympathy for the treatment model than might have been expected. They therefore neither saw probation orders made under this dispensation as being better alternatives to custody than 'traditional' orders, nor, on the whole, made probation orders significantly more frequently than they had in the past.

There are as yet no published reports on the operation of any probation offices working formally to the 'Non-Treatment Paradigm', so we must try to draw a more general conclusion from this one study alone. This conclusion must be that, whatever other advantages it offers, being more explicit about the formal conditions in probation orders does not necessarily enhance the orders as alternatives to custody in the eyes of those passing sentence. Indeed, one might speculate that the purely voluntary offer and acceptance of help used in this scheme is less attractive to the courts than more traditional orders where the mixture of care and control may be seen as ensuring that the offender gets the help, or treatment, that he or she is seen to need.

Similarly, Bottoms and McWilliams' proposal to shift the emphasis on diversion from custody by the probation service away from the provision of extra facilities and towards officers' practices in making recommendations in SIRs may make only a limited contribution to changing the sentencing practices of the courts.

It may indeed be true that recommendations in SIRs can persuade sentencers, particularly magistrates, to deal with offenders more harshly than they would otherwise have done,[24] but it is at least arguable that it is not the making of custodial recommendations, but the very process of preparing SIRs, that gives courts the authority to impose custodial sentences.[25]

In this process the perceived role of the treatment ideology is important. Pauline Hardiker[26] has argued from her study of a probation intake team in Leicestershire that a 'treatment orientation' – that is to say one that involves an assessment of an offender's need for social work – is a valuable modifier of the justice element in social inquiry reports. She argues that, through this, probation can be seen as particularly appropriate for those in high need, even though custody may often be recognized as unavoidable and appropriate for serious offenders lacking such needs. She also points out that research suggests that more serious offenders tend to have greater personal needs. From this one can argue that the retention of the treatment model in probation may tend overall to divert offenders from custody, even if there is a danger that custodial recommendations in SIRs may in fact divert individual offenders in the opposite direction.

This argument has recently been criticized[27] as offering a misleading model of the ways in which probation officers come to make recommendations in reports, and in which magistrates receive them. These criticisms have subsequently been answered.[28] Our own view is that apparent problems in validating the 'reverse tariff' hypothesis advanced by Hardiker may in fact be related to changes in probation practice in response to the general assault on the idea of 'treatment' which may, in some senses, be seen as culminating in the 'Non-Treatment Paradigm'. In brief, it is possible that probation officers, with the treatment ideology apparently deflated, and faced with an increasingly bleak social environment and outlook for their clients, have been making more modest assessments of the help they can give to clients, and therefore of the needs they can appropriately meet. As there does appear to be a link between high social need and frequency or seriousness of offending, such a decline in officers' aspirations may make them less likely to recommend probation than they or their predecessors were when the treatment ideal was paramount.

At the moment this hypothesis has not been tested against empirical evidence, but research into the actual practice of probation officers supervising clients does seem to support the proposition that if there ever were a treatment orientation it is now much weaker. Andrew Willis, reporting in the *British Journal of Social Work*[29] on an observational study made in 1979 of the interaction between probationers and their supervising officers, concluded that, while clients found their contact with probation officers helpful and valuable, their experiences bore little relation to the treatment ideal and more relation (even in 1979) to the kind of practice advocated in the 'Non-Treatment Paradigm'. Willis himself depicts this as 'a grass roots, practice response to collapse of confidence in the treatment model'.[30]

One question that emerges here is how, and why, did the treatment model 'collapse'. We have already referred to criticisms and critiques of it, but it is also important to describe and comment on the relevant antecedent arguments in some detail.

Criticisms of the treatment ideal have taken two main forms: that it is unjust, and that it does not work. The accusation of injustice was in fact applied principally to treatment as it was used in the American prison system, and it is worth noting that one of its main exponents, von Hirsh,[31] appears to regard probation as an unwelcome anomaly in his description of just and unjust sentences. Nevertheless, it can be said that probation is potentially unjust, in that the probation officer has a great deal of discretion as to whether or not to bring an offender back to court for failing to comply with the conditions of the order. It is also unjust in that it is probable that not all probation officers are equally good at working with all clients and, therefore, in theory at least, an offender who is supervised by the 'wrong' officer, and who does not realize his right to apply to change officers, can be penalized by receiving inappropriate treatment, which may *increase* his chances of reoffending. There is some evidence from research into probation work, and from the annual statistics prepared by the Home Office about the work of the probation service, which bears on these two issues of justice.

The probation statistics[32] suggest that officers' discretion in bringing clients back to court, while it may disadvantage some individuals, acts to the benefit of the majority. Of some 38,000 probation orders ending in 1982, 14 per cent were terminated early for 'good progress' or replaced by a conditional discharge, 2 per cent were terminated prematurely for failing to comply with the requirements of the order, 2 per cent were terminated for other reasons, and 14 per cent were terminated for reoffending. In perhaps 1 per cent of orders that ran their full course a breach of probation for failing to comply with the order was proved but not acted on by the court. It seems probable, however, that rather more than four clients in every hundred are *technically*, although not seriously, in breach of the requirements of an order even though they do not reoffend, and therefore that the discretion of probation officers acts more to keep clients on supervision than to expose them to the risk of receiving sentences which may or may not be more severe than probation. One might argue, therefore, that the exercise of discretion, while unjust in theory, may be more beneficial than otherwise in practice.

The second point about justice relates to the individual relationship between probation officer and client, and the way in which this can be harmful or helpful. This is a special case of what is called in the research literature an 'interaction effect'. The basic theory of interaction effects (or 'interactionism'), as it is usually applied in criminological research, is that a particular form of intervention or sentence will be effective with some types of offender, but ineffective or counterproductive with others, as a product of the interaction between the offender and the intervention.[33]

There is some evidence for the existence of general interaction effects, of which the most relevant to the probation order is that found in the IMPACT study.[34] This research project, run by the Home Office Research Unit, had as its main objective to compare the effectiveness of intensive and ordinary probation supervision for 'high risk' cases. No overall difference in effectiveness was found between the two types of probation, but the research did indicate that different types of offender responded differently to them – in particular, more 'criminal' offenders with few personal problems did better under ordinary supervision, while less 'criminal' ones with more personal problems appeared to do better under intensive supervision. Other research studies in the criminological and other fields suggest an interaction between client and worker.[35] We can therefore say that there *is* evidence of interaction effects, and therefore of the possibility of injustice within a treatment setting.

Against this, however, we must point out that the potential for such injustice is inherent in any situation involving interpersonal relationships, and that this criticism of treatment applies equally to any model of probation involving the provision of 'help', unless that help is impersonal and bureaucratized.

Furthermore, it is arguable that the probation service has developed, and is developing, ways of working which meet these criticisms of injustice. Phyllida Parsloe[36] has argued that the supervision of probation officers by more senior or probation officers acts as a helpful restraint on individual workers' exercise of discretion, and that this restraint acts in the clients' interests. Thus, supervision by senior staff should prevent officers from acting arbitrarily and unjustly towards their clients. In addition, the term 'probation' covers in practice a multiplicity of styles of work – from help, advocacy and crisis intervention to 'deep casework', and from one-to-one supervision in the office to group 'adventure activities' at sea or in the mountains. As most of these alternatives are often available within or accessible to any probation office, there is considerable opportunity for clients to be involved, if appropriate, in different kinds of interventions and experiences. It must be said, however, that some probation teams are organized to facilitate this process rather better than are others (and perhaps the majority). Finally, as we have observed, it is possible for clients to transfer from one probation officer to another.

We would not claim that the practices and possibilities briefly outlined above constitute a full answer to criticisms of injustice in the application of probation orders – indeed many of them are founded on the same kinds of feelings about 'traditional' probation as inform the criticisms of treatment in general. We would argue, nevertheless, that they show that it is possible for probation to change without moving to the extremes of a 'justice' model. It seems, therefore, that while there are some reasons for saying that the theory of probation is unjust, these injustices may be very much less severe in practice than theory predicts.

There remains, however, the criticism that treatment does not work. This can be interpreted in two ways – that treatment is ineffective in producing desirable outcomes (particularly a reduction in the likelihood of reoffending) and that treatment makes no contribution to diverting offenders from prison. The research evidence for these contentions is not, however, as compelling as might be expected.

In the criminological field, the first significant and widely publicized claim that treatment, both in and out of custody, did not work was made by the late Dr Robert Martinson. In 1974 he published in America an article entitled 'What Works? Questions and Answers about Prison Reform',[37] in which he concluded that virtually no form of 'correctional treatment' (i.e. the treatment of offenders in custody or in the community) was effective. Martinson's views were softened somewhat in a book he co-authored with Lipton and Wilks – *The Effectiveness of Correctional Treatment: A Survey of Treatment Evaluation Studies* (1975)[38] – which was based, as was the original article, on a review of some 286 research studies into the effectiveness of 'treatment programs' applied to offenders, carried out between 1945 and 1968.

This work was repeated in England by Stephen Brody of the Home Office Research Unit, and his 1976 paper[39] appeared to come to the same conclusions as did Martinson, namely that no form of treatment of offenders was demonstrably successful in reducing reconviction rates.[40]

Martinson's and Brody's conclusions found ready acceptance in England and the United States. Lillyquist reports that Martinson's first article was followed in the USA by

> a dramatic shift in both public attitudes and in the pronouncements of correctional officials. It was proclaimed that treatment had failed and that we should return to the more punitive approaches of days past.[41]

In England, where the treatment ideology had not been adopted so wholeheartedly by the criminal justice system, the response was perhaps less vocal, but nevertheless probably as strong, and it seems likely that the 'nothing works' view has helped to confirm rather than to change the sentencing policies of judges and magistrates.

One of the few early dissentients from the new orthodoxy was

Palmer who, in 1975, criticized the conclusions of 'What Works?'[42] Palmer's criticisms are developed and summarized in his 1978 book *Correctional Intervention and Research* in which, in particular, he observes with some justice that Martinson's pronouncements on the subject went at times somewhat beyond the limits of reasonable conclusions from his data. Palmer also suggested that Martinson was being too severe in accepting as evidence of effectiveness only general treatment effects, and ignoring projects which apparently worked for some offenders but not for others. Thus, he suggested, many promising leads for future 'treatment programs' might be unfairly neglected.[43] This is an important point, in that both Brody's and Martinson's observations are more hopeful for the probation order than they appeared at first sight.

We can in fact conclude from the material that Martinson and Brody have presented that:

1. There is no evidence that probation is *less* effective than custody and some (tenuous) suggestions that it can be better at preventing reconviction.

2. There is evidence that some projects do work with some people; some workers achieve better results than others and differential effects on different types of client have also been observed; there are also indications from studies of treatment in custodial and residential institutions that a project based on individual assessment may produce benefits. The difficulty is that to date little evidence has been produced about why some projects might work and others not.

3. The research designs used in the studies observed developed several difficulties in practice, which have rendered many of the results questionable. The conclusion that 'nothing works' is not the only one that can be derived from these questions.

4. While there is no consistent pattern of outcomes for probation, possibly because the objectives of the studies have not been consistent, there are several methodological reasons why this might be so:

   (a) In many studies sample sizes were too small for significant results to be achieved and the results that were seen may have been wrongly discounted because they could not be statistically significant.[44] As it can be argued that the impact of casework on reoffending, while important, can only be marginal, it may be suggested that some at least of the projects which returned 'poor' results were setting unrealistic goals.

(b) Insufficient attention was often paid in these studies to the processes by which social work intervention might produce the desired results.

(c) The operational differences between experimental and control groups may often have been imprecise and less strong or certain than had been claimed or intended.

(d) Not all the intervention strategies ascribed to the experimental groups were appropriate to the problems faced by clients.

(e) 'Global' treatment effects were studied and perhaps insufficient attention was paid in the initial designs to interaction effects.

Not all these criticisms are applicable to every study reported on by Brody and Martinson (in IMPACT, for example, special attention was paid to interaction effects), but most of the studies can be criticized under at least one of these headings.

Thus while the evidence that has been collected so far about the effectiveness of treatment does not support some of the more exaggerated claims that have been made for it, equally it does not lend weight to a total devaluation of probation.

It is noteworthy that the problems that have been encountered in evaluating the effect of probation also occurred in studies of other forms of social work within other agencies. A common issue here is that it can be argued that in all such agencies casework has been overvalued at the cost of other forms of intervention. Probation work, however, has been associated with the idea of change in the subject and the concept of this change leading to a reduction in offending behaviour is at the core of most, if not all, of the evaluation that has been conducted. The proportion of offenders for whom change is a viable proposition may, however, be relatively small, particularly if such work is focused on those who have identified problems to be worked on in collaboration with the probation officer. Intervention by social workers and probation officers can have a variety of objectives and modes, however, of which work orientated towards change is only one. Thus, a research project in an English social services department[45] showed that in 40 per cent of ongoing family cases and 50 per cent of cases of mental illness or emotional disturbance, no change was intended by the social worker during the coming year. The same study showed that in 31 per cent of current and recently closed family cases, and 36 per cent of cases of mental illness, etc., the social worker had been substantially involved in sustaining and supporting the client, while the facilitation of problem-solving or decision-making took place in 52 per cent and 30 per cent respectively of those cases.

In social work too, the conclusions reached from research carried out in the twenty or thirty years after World War II were such as to cast doubts on the effectiveness of social work in general situations as much as in probation. Yet, as Reid and Hanrahan have pointed out,[46] these conclusions may owe as much to the *structure* of the projects researched as they do to the question of effectiveness. By contrast, they argue, more recent research has focused on the achievement by clients through social work intervention of more specific, less general goals over relatively short periods of time. Because the longer-term interaction between clients and their social environment may only be marginally affected by social work after the end of intervention, these studies have not looked for lasting but only immediate treatment effects. This concentration on the immediate and the specific in well-controlled studies has, they suggest, led to a demonstration that social casework is effective, at least within certain boundaries. The research programme that the Home Office Research Unit (now the Research and Planning Unit) began in the 1960s and of which the IMPACT study appears to be the pinnacle, might usefully have been extended along the principles outlined by Reid to delineate more clearly those areas and ways in which probation may work.

Thus the view that 'treatment does not work' may well be only partially true. While no single approach to probation supervision has been shown to be universally successful, there are, as we have seen, hints that some kinds of intervention might be successful with certain kinds of offender; there are also indications that approaches based on interpersonal relationships between caseworker and client can be at least as effective as other methods.

The argument that probation can act, and has acted in some cases, as an alternative to custody also appears to receive support from reconviction rates of offenders following different sentences.

In 1977 the Home Office completed a study of the reconvictions over a six-year period of a cohort of offenders sentenced in November 1971. This study suggested that much of the variation in reconviction rates for different sentences was attributable to the different levels of criminality – as measured by the number of previous convictions – of those sentenced. Overall, the report suggested that there was no association between sentence and reconviction – in other words, all sentences were about equally effective or ineffective at preventing reconviction.[47]

A reanalysis of this data at the Cambridge Institute of Criminology, reported in the *British Journal of Criminology*,[48] cast doubt on this assertion, at least as far as adult males were concerned. Looking at the reconviction rates of those with the same numbers of previous convictions given different sentences for similar offences, it appeared that there *were* associations between sentence and reconviction, and that these varied according to the length of the offender's previous record. In particular it appeared that probation was:

less effective than imprisonment for first offenders;

more effective than imprisonment for those with 2–4 previous convictions;

as ineffective as imprisonment for those with over 5 previous convictions.

Interpretation of the results was hampered by the relatively small numbers involved, but these figures do suggest both that there is a 'middle-risk' group of offenders for whom probation may have been more effective than prison, and that for 'confirmed' offenders probation is no less effective. The curious finding that imprisonment was more effective than probation for first offenders may be a tribute to its deterrent effects, but is more probably, in our view, a consequence of the fact that, as relatively few adult male first offenders were imprisoned, those who were represented 'special cases'.

It should be noted that these figures describe the outcomes of probation orders made when the ideal of 'treatment' was apparently strong. They appear if anything to confirm rather than deny the appropriateness of social work in probation orders to the sentencing of offenders.

It is tempting, on the basis of the evidence that we have presented about the nature of contemporary practice, to suggest that not only has treatment been supplanted by 'helping' modes of intervention, but also that, as this treatment was neither as ineffective nor as inappropriate as its critics have suggested, this process is damaging the perceived role of the probation order as an alternative to custody.

This may not be a bad thing in itself. Pease[49] has presented the argument, in the context of community service orders and suspended sentences, that introducing new alternatives to custody has had the effect of making the average sentence more severe, and of putting many people in jeopardy of custodial sentences which their offences and records may not merit. A conclusion from this argument is that a wider range of relatively lenient sentences should be promoted to counterbalance this effect, and it may be that the probation order is moving in this direction.

Another effect of the decline of treatment has been a corresponding growth in the demand for more controlling elements in probation orders. This has found expression in the provisions of the 1982 Criminal Justice Act empowering courts to impose requirements in probation orders for the client to attend specified day centres, for example, or to refrain from attending football matches. An earlier and more extreme example is the Kent Control Unit, which probationers were required to attend during the day and in evenings. In the interests of providing courts with an alternative to custody, the Control Unit maintained a regime that contained many of the restrictive elements of a prison sentence.[50]

It may perhaps be a healthy sign that such controlling conditions in probation orders are now more overt than they were in the past, but their presence in part reflects a perceived desire on the part of the courts to have available, within the context of a probation order, a more substantial approach to dealing with clients than just the provision of help.

The difficulty is that if probation seems to become more marginal to offenders' criminal behaviour through the adoption of help as opposed to treatment as its fundamental ideology, and if it continues to be used as an alternative to custody, so the pressure for probation officers to exercise ever more social control over their clients will increase. This tendency has already been noted by other commentators, especially Beaumont and Walker[51] and Willis,[52] but it is difficult to see how, in our present circumstances, it should be reversed. To resurrect the old ideology of treatment seems both impractical and undesirable, but some other alternatives may be suggested.

During the last decade, as the critique of treatment was being mounted, the probation service, recognizing that offenders' needs, whether for help, treatment, advice or support, cannot be met only by individualized long-term casework supervision, has been developing a variety of forms of intervention. These have included probation hostels and day training centres (both used through a condition in a probation order), voluntary day centres, supported work schemes, probation orders based on short-term task-centred casework, group work and social skills training.[53] It is true that some of these forms of intervention, and in particular hostels and day training centres, were developed as alternative forms of treatment, but others appear to have sprung from the critique itself – or from practitioners' responses to it.

It is fair to say that none of these approaches has yet shown itself to be significantly better than expected at reducing the likelihood of probationers' future reoffending, but this is perhaps hardly surprising considering the difficulties attendant on demonstrating such an outcome. It is perhaps more relevant here to note Folkard's observation that successful social work in probation appears to be associated with a reduction in reconviction,[54] and on this basis to welcome these developments, in the hope that they will be properly monitored and their results compared to assist in the identification of the more, and less, promising directions to follow.[55]

The practical implications of these trends are that the probation service is gaining more experience in matching clients and services. Until the implementation of the 1982 Criminal Justice Act much of this was done within the context of an ordinary probation order, although in some areas specific conditions – such as to attend a day centre other than a day training centre – were written into orders. By enabling courts to include more specific positive or negative conditions in probation orders, the Act may have the effect of unduly formalizing this matching process and confusing a judicial and magisterial function (setting appropriate sentences) with a social work one (meeting needs), but if this pitfall can be avoided, then there seems no reason why the value to offenders, and to society, of probation orders should not be maintained or enhanced.

For this to happen, some more clarity about the achievements of probation and the means by which these come about seems in order. We must remember that, considered either as a rehabilitative sentence or as a form of control, the probation order appears in general to be at least as effective as any other sentence (including custody) for the first aim, and as good as any other non-custodial sentence for the second. Probation officers achieve these results with relatively little intervention. In the IMPACT experiment, for example, clients receiving experimental, intensive, supervision were seen on average about three times a month, typically for about forty minutes at a time (i.e. a total of about two hours' contact a month). Clients in the control group, receiving ordinary supervision, were seen once or twice a month on average; no data were given for lengths of contact but it seems unlikely that individual sessions were any longer.[56] In judging these figures, it must be remembered that there is a body of evidence, summarized in Martinson, that more contact between supervisor and client results in more revocations of orders,[57] while on the social work side, Reid's work on short- and long-term cases appears to show that more input does not make for better results.[58] (There is an apparent exception to this in that *short-term*, more intensive and focused forms of intervention also seem to achieve satisfactory results; but this is probably because they are both *short-term* and focused – lengthening the intervention or broadening its goals appears to be an unproductive exercise.)

What this means in general terms is that there is no evidence that more social control exercised by probation officers (nor, less relevantly in this argument, more social work) will produce any better results in terms of revoked orders and reconvicted probationers than are currently achieved. Furthermore, it is at least worth exploring the possibility that less structure in the conditions of probation orders, and more scope for the exercise of professional judgement within probation services would, once the damaging myths about control have gone the way of those about treatment, help courts again to use the probation order as an alternative to custody.

In this context, it is interesting to see how the conditions of hostel residence, and of day training centre attendance, in probation orders have developed. The idea of both probation hostels and day training centres was based on the principle that some categories of offenders need more supportive and structured non-custodial environments in which they can be treated, trained or helped to adjust to society. Following a recommendation in the 1967 *Report on Non-Custodial and Semi-Custodial Penalties*, the system of probation hostels, originally developed to deal with young offenders, was expanded to provide for adults. Currently some 1,600 probation orders each year (5 per cent of the total) contain a requirement to reside in a probation hostel (*c.* 1,200 cases) or in some other residential establishment (*c.* 400).[59]

Research in the 1960s into probation hostels cast doubt on the value, and indeed the reality, of the treatment regimes operating in them; hostels appeared to derive their effectiveness more from the personalities of key members of staff. Furthermore, it was difficult to see any obvious rehabilitative effects – as measured by reconviction rates – on former residents of hostels; it appeared that social skills and attitudes learned in the hostel were not necessarily transferable to the outside world. Thus in general the concept of the hostel as an environment for treatment was called into question.[60] On the other hand, research into the needs of offenders has identified lack of stable accommodation as a key variable associated with offending,[61] and so the value of probation hostels in giving primary supportive care to their residents is coming to be recognized more overtly. A research study in Inner London, looking at the attitudes of residents towards their probation hostels, has shown the value that they put on attributes such as privacy, and suggests that probation hostels can play a role in providing a second-best substitute for a 'real home'.[62]

The history of day training centres shows a different kind of shift away from treatment ideals. Four experimental centres were set up following the 1973 Criminal Justice Act, and were originally intended to provide basic training in 'living skills' for socially inadequate offenders at risk of custodial sentences. The four centres – in London, Sheffield, Liverpool and Pontypridd – all developed individually distinct ways of working, linked mainly by the day training centre requirement in probation orders – to attend a centre for a period of sixty days. It would be fair to say that all the centres dealt with more serious offenders, at risk of longer custodial sentences, than had been originally envisaged. In this they were encouraged by being promoted as alternatives to custody for the use of the Crown Court.

An evaluation study of these centres by the Home Office Research Unit was set up, but little was in fact published from this; some internal evaluations, by the probation areas containing the centres, were also carried out, however, and these demonstrated the centres' ability to provide a non-custodial alternative sufficiently well to impress both the House of Commons Expenditure Committee on reducing the prison population[63] and the May inquiry into the prisons. Certainly there is no evidence that day training centres were any less effective than their contemporary non-custodial alternative, community service (see Chapter 5).

Day training centres, however, laboured under two disadvantages. Firstly, they were, or appeared to be, relatively expensive; the Inner London centre had an establishment of one senior probation officer and six probation officers to work with between 20 and 30 clients at one time – a total intake of 80 to 90 a year – and was reputed to cost as much a week per head as did prison.[64] (This equivalence leaves aside the social costs and benefits of custody against freedom.) Secondly, the work of the centres was based on the idea of treatment, and continued to be so even when that idea fell out of favour. Finally, as Vanstone and Raynor suggest,[65] the centres may have suffered, paradoxically, from keeping strictly to the idea that they did present only an alternative to custody.

While the four 'experimental' centres were operating, the provision of voluntary day centres was also developing, and in time these came to be used as resources for the courts in sentencing. Thus some courts began to insert conditions of attending day centres – from the extreme of the Kent Control Unit to much less structured establishments – into probation orders, sometimes with the intention of providing help for offenders, sometimes to obtain a greater measure of control over them. The legality of these conditions of day centre attendance (when the day centre was not a specified day training centre) was queried and it was held that in fact courts could only insert a condition of day centre attendance in a probation order when it referred to one of the four 'experimental' centres. This position held until the implementation of the 1982 Criminal Justice Act, which gave courts a wider power to impose conditions of probation such as day centre attendance, and effectively abolished the particular status of day training centres.

NOTES AND REFERENCES

1 L. Radzinowicz, *The Results of Probation*, London: Macmillan, 1958, p. xii.

2 A.E. Bottoms and W. McWilliams, 'A Non-Treatment Paradigm for Probation Practice', *British Journal of Social Work*, Vol. 9, 1979, pp. 159–202.

3 See, for example, the statistics quoted in D. Haxby, *Probation, A Changing Service*, London: Constable, 1978, pp. 301–14.

4 L. Radzinowicz, *The Results of Probation*, op. cit.

5 Home Office, *Criminal Statistics, England and Wales 1981*, London: HMSO, 1982.

6 Ibid. It must be remembered, of course, that during this period the probation service also took on additional responsibilities, in particular for the after-care of prisoners and for running community service schemes.

7 D. Bochel, *Probation and After-Care: Its Development in England and Wales*, Edinburgh: Scottish Academic Press, 1976.

8 One alternative proposal was that policemen should act as probation officers; however, this was judged to be incompatible with their other duties. See D. Bochel, *Probation and After-Care*, op. cit., Chapter 1.

9 Inner London Probation and After-Care Service, *ILPAS'76: A Report on Aspects of the Work of the Inner London Probation and After-Care Service*, London: ILPAS, 1976.

10 Quoted in D. Bochel, *Probation and After-Care*, op. cit., p. 34.

11 Ibid., p. 48.

12 Ibid., p. 50.

13 Ibid., p. 63.

14 P. Parsloe, 'Issues of Social Control', in J.F.S. King (ed.), *Pressures and Change in the Probation Service*, Cambridge: University of Cambridge Institute of Criminology, Cropwood Conference Series No. 11, 1979.

15 See D. May, 'Delinquency and the Treatment Model', *British Journal of Criminology*, Vol. 11, 1971, p. 361.

16 See, for example, National Association of Probation Officers, *The Provision of Alternatives to Custody and the Use of the Probation Order*, London: NAPO, 1981. This argument of course assumes that the rational decision is the one that leads to self-reform. It holds true, however, even if offenders have been making rational decisions to offend; it is unreasonable to expect them suddenly to become (by their standards) irrational.

17 P. Parsloe, 'Issues of Social Control', op. cit.

18 M. Bryant, J. Coker, B. Estlea, S. Himmel and T. Knapp, 'Sentenced to Social Work?' *Probation Journal*, Vol. 25, 1978, pp. 110–14.

19 R.D. Colley *et al.*, 'Administration and Individual Responsibility', *Probation*, Vol. 16, quoted in D. Haxby, *Probation, a Changing Service*, op. cit.

20 A.E. Bottoms and W. McWilliams, 'A Non-Treatment Paradigm for Probation Practice', op. cit.

21 Ibid., p. 172.

22 Ibid., p. 186.

23 B. Sheppard, 'Monitoring Two New Approaches in Hampshire', *Justice of the Peace*, Vol. 146, No. 37, 1982, pp. 560–2.

24 See J. Hine, W. McWilliams and K. Pease, 'Recommendations, Social Information and Sentencing', *Howard Journal*, Vol. 17, No. 2, 1978, pp. 91–100.

25 See J. Roberts and C. Roberts, 'Social Enquiry Reports and Sentencing', *Howard Journal*, Vol. 21, No. 2, 1982, pp. 76–93, for a discussion of the relationship (or lack of it) between SIR recommendations and magistrates' courts' sentencing patterns.

26 See especially P. Hardiker, 'Social Work Ideologies in the Probation Service', *British Journal of Social Work*, Vol. 7, No. 22, 1977, pp. 131–54, and P. Hardiker, 'The Role of Probation Officers in Sentencing', in H. Parker (ed.), *Social Work and the Courts*, London: Edward Arnold, 1979, pp. 117–34.

27 J. Paley and R. Leeves, 'Some Questions about the Reverse Tariff', *British Journal of Social Work*, Vol. 12, No. 4, 1982, pp. 363–80.

28 D. Webb and P. Hardiker, 'In Defence of the Reverse Tariff: A Response to Paley and Leeves,' *British Journal of Social Work*, Vol. 13, No. 2, 1983, pp. 207–18.

29 A. Willis, 'The Balance between Care and Control in Probation: A Research Note', *British Journal of Social Work*, Vol. 13, No. 3, 1983, pp. 339–46.

30 Ibid., p. 345.

31 A. von Hirsh, *Doing Justice: The Choice of Punishments*, Toronto: McGraw-Hill Ryerson Ltd, 1976.

32 Home Office, *Probation Statistics, England and Wales 1982*, London: Home Office, 1984.

33 For a brief summary of the interactionist perspective see M. Lillyquist, *Understanding and Changing Criminal Behavior*, New Jersey: Prentice-Hall, 1980, pp. 15–21.

34 The IMPACT study is reported in detail in M.S. Folkard *et al.*, *Intensive Matched Probation and After-Care Treatment*, Vol. I: *The Design of the Probation Experiment and an Interim Evaluation*, Home Office Research Study No. 24, London: HMSO, 1974; Vol. II: *The Results of the Experiment*, Home Office Research Study No. 26, London: HMSO, 1976. There is also a thought-provoking discussion by M.S. Folkard, 'Second Thoughts on IMPACT', in E.M. Goldberg and N. Connelly (eds), *Evaluative Research in Social Care*, London: Heinemann Educational, 1981.

35 See M. Lillyquist, *Understanding and Changing Criminal Behavior*, op. cit., and also C.B. Truax and R.R. Carckhoff, *Toward Effective Counseling and Psychotherapy*, Chicago: Aldine Publishing Co., 1967.

36 P. Parsloe, 'Issues of Social Control', op. cit.

37 R. Martinson, 'What Works? Questions and Answers about Prison Reform', *The Public Interest*, No. 35, 1974, pp. 22–54.

38 D. Lipton, R. Martinson and J. Wilks, *The Effectiveness of Correctional Treatment: A Survey of Treatment Evaluation Studies*, New York: Praeger, 1975.

39 S.R. Brody, *The Effectiveness of Sentencing*, Home Office Research Study No. 32, London: HMSO, 1976.

40 The question of the value of reconviction as a measure of the failure of a particular sentence or project is one that has been much discussed. Despite the problem that a reconviction may have little to do with whether an offender has 'reformed', the unfortunate fact remains that it is the only measure that can be used consistently in this area because it is the only measure available that relates to the general objectives of sentencing and intervention after sentence. In any case, as Folkard ('Second Thoughts on IMPACT', op. cit.) points out, avoidance of reconviction is generally strongly associated with other successful treatment outcomes: in other

words, people who improve in other ways do not usually reoffend (or if they do, they don't get caught).

41 M. Lillyquist, *Understanding and Changing Criminal Behavior*, op. cit, p. 18.

42 T. Palmer, 'Martinson Revisited', *Journal of Research in Crime and Delinquency*, Vol. 12, 1975, pp. 133–92.

43 T. Palmer, *Correctional Intervention and Research*, Lexington and Toronto: D.C. Heath & Co., 1979.

44 Other commentators, such as Dr Ken Pease, have pointed this out, but, so far as we know, none have committed their observation to print. In statistical terms, this is an example of a 'Type 2' error, *rejecting* the hypothesis that there is a difference when there is one in fact, even though the sample studied does not show the difference to be significant, because the sample is too small to do otherwise. The only remedies appear to be to increase the sample size or refine the hypothesis being tested. As the former is difficult to achieve, much current research appears to be moving in the latter direction.

45 E.M. Goldberg and W. Warburton, *Ends and Means in Social Work*, London: Allen & Unwin, 1978.

46 W.J. Reid and P. Hanrahan, 'The Effectiveness of Social Work: Recent Evidence', 'The Evaluation of Social Work', in E.M. Goldberg and N. Connelly (eds), *Evaluative Research in Social Care*, op. cit.

47 G.J.O. Philpotts and L.B. Lancucki, *Previous Convictions, Sentence and Reconviction*, Home Office Research Study No. 53, London: HMSO, 1979.

48 N. Walker, D.P. Farrington and G. Tucker, 'Reconviction Rates of Adult Males after Different Sentences', *British Journal of Criminology*, Vol. 21, No. 4, 1981, pp. 357–60.

49 K. Pease, 'Community Service and Prison: Are They Alternatives?', in K. Pease and W. McWilliams (eds), *Community Service by Order*, Edinburgh: Scottish Academic Press, 1980.

50 See A. Mills, 'Controversy on the Medway', *Probation Journal*, Vol. 28, No. 3, 1981, pp. 80–5.

51 B. Beaumont and H. Walker, *Probation Work: Critical Theory and Socialist Practice*, Oxford: Basil Blackwell, 1981.

52 A. Willis, 'The Balance between Care and Control in Probation', op. cit.

53 See, for example, National Probation Research and Information Exchange, *Index of Probation Projects 1982–83*, London: Home Office, 1983, and also D.A. Millard, 'Broader Approaches to Probation Practice', in J.F.S. King (ed.), *Pressures and Change in the Probation Service*, op. cit.

54 M.S. Folkard, 'Second Thoughts on IMPACT', op. cit.

55 T. Palmer, *Correctional Intervention and Research*, op. cit.

56 M.S. Folkard, *Intensive Matched Probation and After-Care Treatment*, Vol. II: *The Results of the Experiment*, op. cit.

57 D. Lipton *et al., The Effectiveness of Correctional Treatment*, op. cit.

58 W.J. Reid and A.W. Shyne, *Brief and Extended Casework*, New York and London: Columbia University Press, 1969; W.J. Reid and L. Epstein, *Task-Centered Casework*, New York and London: Columbia University Press, 1972; W.J. Reid, *The Task-Centered System*, New York and Guildford: Columbia University Press, 1978.

59 Home Office, *Probation Statistics, England and Wales 1982*, op. cit.

60 See I. Sinclair and R. Clarke, 'Cross-Institutional Designs', in E.M. Goldberg and N. Connelly (eds), *Evaluative Research in Social Care*, op. cit.

61 See S. Fairhead, *Persistent Petty Offenders*, Home Office Research Study No. 66, London: HMSO, 1981.

62 P. Maitland and R. Woodward, *Research into the Perceptions of Hostel Residents*, London: ILPS, 1983.

63 See House of Commons Fifteenth Report from the Expenditure Committee, Session 1977–1978, *The Reduction of Pressure on the Prison System*, London: HMSO, 1978, Vol. II, paras 188–92.

64 S. Shaw, *Paying the Penalty: An Analysis of the Cost of Penal Sanctions*, London: NACRO, 1980.

65 M. Vanstone and P. Raynor, 'Diversion from Prison – Partial Success and a Missed Opportunity', *Probation Journal*, Vol. 28, No. 3, 1981, pp. 85–9.

Chapter Five

THE NEW ALTERNATIVES

The decline in the courts' use of probation orders as an alternative to imprisonment has been accompanied, over the last fifteen years, by the introduction of a variety of new sentencing options, all intended to divert offenders from custody, and all failing, to greater or lesser extents, to do so.

The first of these alternatives was the suspended sentence. This was introduced in the 1967 Criminal Justice Act as an attempt to achieve the supposed deterrent effect of a short or medium-length custodial sentence without increasing the prison population. When passing a sentence of up to two years' imprisonment, the sentencing court is empowered to *suspend* the introduction of that sentence for a period (also up to two years). If the offender is not reconvicted within the period of suspension, then he or she remains free. If, however, he or she does reoffend and commits an offence punishable with imprisonment within the period of suspension, then the sentencing court can activate the sentence that was suspended.

It was hoped that the introduction of this provision would provide courts with an alternative way of dealing with some of those offenders they were already sending to prison. Its effect, however, seems to have been to have put more people at risk of a prison sentence. Let us look, for example, at its effect on the sentencing practices of magistrates' courts.

Whereas in 1967 only 17 per cent of offenders sentenced by magistrates' courts received an immediate custodial sentence or were committed for sentence to a higher court (in the expectation that they would receive a harsher penalty than the committing court could impose), in 1968 27 per cent received an immediate or suspended custodial sentence or were committed for sentence. Of these, 14 per cent had received a suspended sentence; nevertheless the total proportion of offenders *at risk of prison* had risen by 10 per cent.

We can also estimate where these cases came from. The percentage of offenders receiving fines fell from 62 per cent to 53 per cent, of those put on probation from 10 per cent to 8 per cent, and of those receiving immediate custodial sentences from 13 per cent to 8 per cent. Thus it appears that only about a third of those getting a suspended sentence of imprisonment in 1968 would have received a custodial sentence the previous year. (This figure is calculated by taking the fall in custodial sentences (5 per cent) as a proportion of the percentage of suspended sentences (14 per cent).) By contrast, the same figures suggest that over half would have been fined, and about one in seven put on probation.[1]

It is of course possible to challenge these figures and to argue that the changes in magistrates' sentencing practices between 1967 and 1968 were also caused by changes in the type of offender or offence they were dealing with, but this in fact seems unlikely. Inspection of the yearly criminal statistics published by HMSO[2] suggests that the courts' sentencing practices, as seen in the proportions of offenders receiving different sentences, do not change very much from year to year *except* when changes in the law suddenly alter the options available to them. Therefore we can conclude that the impact of the suspended sentence on magistrates' sentencing practices is adequately described by the statistics we have just quoted. They, in turn, show that from the year of its introduction as an alternative to imprisonment, the suspended sentence in the magistrates' courts was a failure because, although it reduced the number of immediate custodial sentences by a third, it also put at risk of imprisonment about 10 per cent of offenders who would otherwise have been fined or put on probation.

We have already seen that, overall, offenders' chances of being reconvicted do not vary greatly according to the sentence they receive[3] and we would therefore expect about half of those getting a suspended sentence to be reconvicted within two years. About a third of the suspended sentences imposed are activated, and some of these would be cases where the offender's new offence would not, if considered on its own, warrant imprisonment; furthermore, some of these would be offenders who would *not* have received custodial sentences for their earlier offence had the suspended sentence not been available. Thus the net effect of the suspended sentence would be to put into prison some offenders who would not otherwise have been there.

It may be objected that this argument is hypothetical in the extreme, and indeed it is, since, apart from Philpotts and Lancucki's study,[4] nothing has been published about the process by which one sentence is followed, in an offender's career, by another. The *Criminal Statistics*, however, do suggest that part of the rise in prison sentences in the early 1970s was due to the activation of suspended sentences – and if this process put into prison offenders for whom custody was not their 'just deserts' then it should be condemned.

The argument presented here has been substantiated from other sources and by other methods. Sparks[5] estimated that only 40 per cent of those receiving suspended sentences would have been at risk of custody if the law had not been changed, and a subsequent analysis by the Home Office[6] produced an estimate of between 40 and 50 per cent. While these figures are somewhat less pessimistic than our calculation of one-third (of suspended sentences imposed in magistrates' courts), the difference between them is not significant in this argument. Indeed Sparks also estimates that, because the suspended sentence was 'misused', the initial net saving in the prison population was relatively small (about 2,000 admissions in the three-year period 1968–71) and, as we have seen, it is difficult to see that there is now any saving or reduction at all arising from the suspended sentence.

To say that the suspended sentence was 'misused' may be misleading. There is little doubt that its effect on courts' sentencing policies was not at all what its devisers and Parliament had intended but, by introducing a new sentence as a direct alternative to custody, they had unwittingly changed the whole sentencing structure. As has been observed, the effect of introducing a new sentence into the tariff is to draw off cases from sentences *above and below* the new one.[7] If the sentence is seen as being about half-way between the next more severe and less severe disposals, then one would expect it to take cases equally from each of them; if it is seen as being closer to one sentence than to others, then it is likely to take cases more from that sentence, in proportion to how close it is seen to be to it. If the new sentence is seen as at the same level as an existing one, then it will probably take all its cases from that sentence. These principles are fairly well known in the business world, where one important element of marketing strategy is to 'place' your own product in relation to its competitors, to maximize your chances of taking sales from them. Unfortunately, Parliament's understanding of the criminal justice 'market' in 1967 appears to have been insufficient.

The suspended sentence was intended to be placed very close to immediate imprisonment on the tariff. The figures suggest, however, that sentencers saw it as being roughly half-way between imprisonment on the one hand and fines and probation on the other, and probably closer to the latter two than to the former.[8]

This argument is important because the fate of the suspended sentence can be seen as a model, and a warning, for other attempts to promote alternatives to custody by inserting new sentences into the tariff.

That the lesson was learned by some MPs was shown by the response of the House of Commons Expenditure Committee to a

NACRO proposal for a new non-custodial court order; they said, in effect, that the further proliferation of alternatives was undesirable.[9] The recent (1982) introduction of the partially suspended sentence, however, may prove equally disastrous.

The power of the courts to suspend a part of a prison sentence, but to require the offender to serve the first part of it, was included in the 1977 Criminal Law Act (Section 47), but was not immediately available to the courts as this section of the Act was not implemented. One of the reasons for this seems to have been a fear that courts would use this power to give offenders 'a taste of prison' when they would not have imposed a full immediate prison sentence. In 1981 the Home Office *Review of Parole*,[10] which also introduced the idea of 'supervised remission' for short-term prisoners, used this argument against the partially suspended sentence. We shall discuss the history of 'supervised remission' in more detail in the next chapter; here we need only note that it was put forward by the Home Office as a way to reduce the prison population, but was rejected by the Home Secretary after consultation with the various bodies in the criminal justice system, including the judiciary and the probation service.

Despite its earlier doubts, the Government *did* introduce the partially suspended sentence in 1982, apparently as an attempt to achieve the long-term benefits of supervised remission by other means. It was immediately criticized, on the grounds that it is likely to lead to more offenders being jailed, by bodies as diverse as the National Association of Probation Officers, the Justices' Clerks Association and the National Association for the Care and Resettlement of Offenders.[11] NACRO also pointed out that as only sentences of six months or longer can be partially suspended, magistrates may well be encouraged to impose six-month sentences, partially suspended, in cases where at the moment they only award three months' immediate imprisonment, on the grounds that the former would have a greater deterrent effect than the latter, while producing a less immediate burden on the prison system. If, however, partially suspended sentences are activated at the same rate (about a third) as wholly suspended ones, this in turn will lead to more offenders serving longer prison sentences than they would otherwise have done.[12].

By contrast, the Magistrates' Association has commented that the forecast increase in prison sentences 'would only happen if the provisions were misused'.[13] This statement, however, rather misses the point. As we have seen with the suspended sentence (and as we shall also see with community service), the real issue is the way in which the introduction of a new sentence, and particularly one intended to offer a way of reducing the prison population, affects and restructures the whole tariff of sentences available to the courts. Experience suggests that the effects are not always the ones predicted or wished by those who devised or introduced the sentence, and so we await the results of the first year's use of this new option with some anxiety.

In this discussion it is appropriate to quote the Advisory Council on the Penal System's view of the partially suspended sentence in their 1978 report *Sentences of Imprisonment: A Review of Maximum Penalties*.[14] The Advisory Council doubted that the original suspended sentence had reduced the prison population and felt that it may have increased it, firstly because courts used it for offenders who would not otherwise have received custody, and secondly because they had made the suspended sentences *longer* than immediate prison sentences for the same offence would have been. Despite these doubts, the Advisory Council saw the partially suspended sentence as a way of exploiting the research finding that many offenders sent to prison for the first time do not reoffend. They believed, therefore, that it should be used not as a substitute for the suspended sentence, or to give a short sharp shock, but as a sentence for '*serious* first offenders or first-time prisoners *who are bound to have to serve some time in prison* but who may well be . . . deterred by eventually serving only a small part of even the minimum sentence appropriate to the offence' (emphasis added).[15] It seems clear from this that the Advisory Council envisaged a limited and well defined role for the partially suspended sentence. It is not yet clear, however, whether the courts' decisions will accord with the Advisory Council's views.

The current position appears to be summarized in the report of judgement in the case *Regina v Clarke (Linda)* published in *The Times* on 21 May, 1982. In this, the process by which a court should decide on an immediate or suspended prison sentence was set out as follows (emphases added):

> The court should first decide whether a custodial sentence is *necessary*, and make a non-custodial sentence if it is not.
>
> Secondly the court should decide whether a community service order could be made equivalent to the custodial sentence; or whether the *whole* sentence could be suspended. If so then it should make a CSO or suspend the whole sentence.
>
> Thirdly the court should decide what is the shortest sentence that can be imposed. If it is very short then it should be imposed in full, without partial suspension.
>
> Fourthly the court should decide whether the (longer) sentence to be imposed should be partially suspended.

While some readers may find the process difficult to follow, it appears from this that the Appeal Court at any rate sees the partially suspended sentence as lying somewhere between community service and the suspended sentence on the one hand, and immediate imprisonment on the other.

From there we are at present in the realms of speculation. The partially suspended sentence appears to be in the only part of the tariff where it could act to divert offenders from immediate imprisonment. The more like the latter it is seen to be by the courts, the more it will succeed in this, but we still need to ask ourselves whether it is in fact an alternative to custody.

The answer is, of course, that it is not; it is a way of giving offenders short prison sentences – hopefully in the place of longer ones. But, while it may perhaps reduce the prison *population*, there is no reason at all to believe that it will reduce the *number of offenders sent to prison* each year. Indeed, in so far as it may take in cases where a wholly suspended sentence would otherwise have been imposed, it seems entirely possible that the net effect will be an *increase* in the number of custodial sentences imposed. For that reason alone, the partially suspended sentence seems misconceived and if, in addition, the activation rate approaches the third of wholly suspended sentences we suspect that, even if this is not the immediate effect, the result of its introduction will be, within the next two or three years, another increase in the total prison population, even if nothing else changes.

The disadvantages of suspended prison sentences were evident soon after their introduction in 1967. Three years later a sub-committee of the Advisory Council on the Penal System chaired by Baroness Wootton produced a Report on *Non-Custodial and Semi-Custodial Penalties*[16] which was to have a profound impact on the structure of sentencing in England and Wales.

Of the Council's recommendations, six seem particularly significant. They were:

to introduce community service orders;

to give courts the power to defer sentence;

that weekend imprisonment should be used to substitute for continuous custody;

that fine defaulters should not be imprisoned *if* their default was caused by lack of money;

that supervisory orders should be attachable to fines and suspended sentences;

that there should be more probation hostels for adults, and courts should be enabled to order hostel residence without the limitations of a probation order.

Not all these recommendations were accepted and translated into legislation, but the introduction of community service orders, which stemmed from these recommendations, has been regarded, particularly by Governments, as a major step in the provision of alternatives to custody. Before we discuss community service, however, it is worth spending some time looking at the fate of the Council's other recommendations.

Deferred sentences were introduced in the 1972 Criminal Justice Act; the intention was to give the courts the power to defer sentences in cases where an offender's personal circumstances might improve (being about to start a job, for example) and where that improvement was associated by the court with a decrease in the severity of the sentence (presumably on the grounds that, having shown a capacity to change, the person was less likely to reoffend). The period of deferment was also seen as giving the offender an opportunity to compensate the victim of the offence, or otherwise demonstrate his contrition. Thus the power to defer sentence fitted into the model of individualized sentencing, rather than that of 'just deserts', in that the court's decision depended in part at least on how the offender behaved after the offence, and much less on the offence itself.

The power to defer sentence is only dubiously an alternative to custody, as legal precedents appear to limit the courts' ability to impose a custodial sentence after a period of deferment; similarly there are limitations on the courts' power to impose conditions to be observed during deferment. For these reasons deferred sentences offer only limited scope for courts to impose custodial penalties if the 'objectives' of deferment are not met, and also little opportunity for controlling the offender while sentence is deferred. Nevertheless, deferred sentences are used frequently by the courts; there are suggestions that they are used as preludes or alternatives to probation orders, and it could be argued that this provision does give courts the opportunity to sentence offenders lower on the tariff than might otherwise have been the case, and thus may restrict the speed with which some offenders progress to custodial sentences.

Weekend imprisonment has not been introduced as a substitute for continuous custody, although at the time of writing the idea is being discussed afresh. The arguments we have set out about the use of suspended sentences apply equally to weekend imprisonment. It is not a genuine alternative to custody, but an amelioration of its rigours. If it were used *only* to substitute for continuous custody then it should help to reduce the prison population, but experience of the suspended sentence suggests that this would not be the case, and that more, not fewer, offenders would get 'a taste of prison'.

Fine defaulters are still imprisoned. Indeed, approximately a quarter of receptions into custody each year are for default in the payment of a fine. While these represent only a small proportion of the total number of offenders fined each year (about 600,000 plus 1.2 million motoring offenders), they make up a significant proportion of the prison population. A study by Wilkins at Winson Green Prison in 1978 found, for example, that over a quarter of those serving short (six months or less) custodial sentences were fine defaulters.[17]

Imprisonment is available to the courts as a last resort to enforce the payment of fines. Its use is restricted under the 1977 Criminal Law Act to those who fail to pay due to wilful refusal or culpable neglect. The one exception to this is that juvenile offenders cannot be imprisoned for fine default, although their parents or guardians can be, if the court has found it reasonable to make them responsible for payment.[18]

The Winson Green study found that the fines defaulted on ranged from £5 (for being drunk and disorderly) to over £500 for motoring offences and over £900 for theft. A significant proportion, however, were in respect of only minor offences, often committed by 'persistent petty offenders'.[19]

A Home Office Research and Planning Unit study of how fine defaulters were dealt with by some magistrates' courts in South-East England raised questions not only about the extent of the courts' knowledge of offenders' means, but also about the relationship between the fines imposed, the payments ordered and defendants' ability to pay.[20] In this study only about a quarter of the defaulters had an earned income; three out of five were unemployed, and one in eight were housewives, students or retired. The researchers also attempted to relate defaulters' incomes to their needs as defined by the (not particularly generous) supplementary benefits scale. They found that only about a third had more than £5 a week spare after paying for the basic necessities of life, and although the courts apparently took some account of this in setting levels of payment, nevertheless between a third and a half of the defaulters were being asked to pay more than they could afford, and almost half of these were the subject of 'suspended committals' – that is, they would go to prison if they did not pay their arrears.[21]

The two major questions that emerge from those two studies are whether it is in fact necessary to have imprisonment as a last sanction against fine default, and whether courts imposing fines should pay more attention to offenders' ability to pay.

On the first point, it may be conceded that a fine, like any other non-custodial alternative, needs to be supported by the ultimate threat of custody. Wilkins, however, suggested that to deal with defaulters there should be created a separate (imprisonable) offence of refusing to pay a fine though having the means to do so, and also that community service should become available as a sentencing option for fine defaulters.[22]

We have commented elsewhere in this book on the value of placing as many steps as possible in the 'ladder' to a custodial sentence; in the issue of fine enforcement, however, it seems to us that the key question is the amount of the fine imposed in the first place, and the time allowed to pay it.

Fines are commonly regarded as being the most effective and efficient disposal available to the courts, and just under half those sentenced for an indictable offence receive a fine. The Home Office study referred to above, however, contains evidence that some defendants are unable to pay the fine imposed by the court at the rate the court demands. If they are to pay they are faced with a choice between considerable hardship or further offending to get the money they need. In such circumstances it is hardly surprising that questions of unwillingness and inability to pay are far from easy for the courts to disentangle.

A further, but important point is that the impact of the fine on the offender may thus in fact be more severe than the court would consider appropriate for the offence, and therefore that the potential for injustice which critics have discerned in individualized sentences such as probation[23] is also present in the imposition of fines without a proper regard for offenders' ability to pay.

The number of committals to prison for fine default may bear witness, therefore, not only to the perceived incorrigibility of some offenders but also to the inappropriateness of fines as sentences in some cases.

Supervisory orders have been added to fines and to suspended sentences of between six months' and two years' imprisonment, in the shape of money payment supervision orders and suspended sentence supervision orders. Both these orders are used only in a minority of cases, and the latter can be made only where the sentence suspended was over six months. Thus, effectively, it is used only by the Crown Court.

In 1982 nearly 6,000 persons became subject to money payment supervision orders administered by the probation service,[24] and during the same year the probation service recorded the termination of over 5,000 such orders. Of these, more than half (56 per cent) were successful, in that the fine was paid or payment was remitted by the court; in nearly one case in three the order lapsed, the offender disappeared or the order was terminated for other reasons; and in 12 per cent of cases – about 700 persons – the offender was committed to prison in default of paying the fine.[25]

Suspended sentence supervision orders show a relatively higher level of use. In 1982 about 1,800 of these orders were made, and about 1,900 terminated.[26] Over two-thirds of the orders terminated (73 per cent) had run their full course or were terminated early for good progress, and 6 per cent were terminated for other reasons. In over one case in five, however – about 400 persons – the suspended sentence was activated.[27]

As the rate of activation of suspended sentences when a supervision order is made appears to be about the same as the activation rate for all suspended sentences made by the Crown Court (about one-fifth), we may argue that these supervision orders are at least as effective at containing the offenders to whom they apply as are suspended sentences in general. Very little, however, is known about the criteria adopted by judges in deciding whether or not to make a suspended sentence supervision order. One possibility is that the judge decides to impose a suspended sentence and then adds, as it were, a supervision order in cases where it appears that the offender needs help from a probation officer to keep him (five orders out of six are made for male offenders) out of trouble. If this process is followed, then the results suggest that judges are good at identifying a minority of offenders who would benefit from supervision, and that probation officers are good at helping, directly or indirectly, these of their clients to avoid reoffending. It is tempting to go beyond the facts and suggest that there are more offenders receiving suspended sentences who might benefit from the addition of a supervision order to help them avoid a consequent prison sentence. The logical extension of this argument, however, is that if it is the supervision order that diverts people from reoffending, why is the suspended sentence needed? Why should not the court instead make probation orders, which have in theory the same sanctions in imprisonable offences? This brings us to our second process for making suspended sentence supervision orders.

It is possible that, instead of deciding to impose suspended sentences with supervision added, a judge would first decide that in this case supervision by the probation service was appropriate, and *then* impose a suspended sentence as a more certain sanction for reoffending than the general power the court possesses in a probation order to impose a custodial sentence (if appropriate) for the original offence for which the order was made.

We are not suggesting that many, or indeed any, judges do in fact go through this kind of decision process when making a suspended sentence supervision order; there is no evidence either way. We would argue, however, that as the decisions of the court of appeal seem to have made it more difficult for courts to impose custodial sentences for breaches of probation orders, so the temptation to decide on supervision first and then add the sanction of a prison sentence for reoffending must be great. And if the temptation is there to use this order instead of probation, so its effectiveness as an alternative to custody comes increasingly into question, as it may be that an even smaller proportion than 40 or 50 per cent of those subject to it are actually at risk of an immediate prison sentence.

It seems clear from the above discussion that the suspended sentence supervision order can have a potential for diverting more offenders from custody than did the suspended sentence alone. At the same time we have doubts, in the absence of firm evidence, that it is being used in this way.

Probation hostels have been discussed in Chapter 4.

One common feature of all the Advisory Council's recommendations is their reliance on individualized sentencing by the courts. The sum total of their intent appears to have been to expand the range of discretionary sentences available to the courts rather than, as contemporaries in America were beginning to argue, to restrict it to ensure that the same offenders receive the same sentences for the same offences. In this it appears that the Advisory Council's report was one of the last manifestations of a particular era in British penological thinking, rather than a glimmer of the dawn of a new age. One of the sentences they recommended, however, appears to have passed over the gap and to be flourishing, despite many criticisms. That sentence is the community service order.

Community service was described by the Advisory Council as 'the most ambitious proposal' of their report.[28] In the form it was originally proposed it was *not* intended solely as an alternative to custody, but to be used for non-imprisonable offences; it was also intended as a *reformative* sentence, to give an offender an opportunity to change his view of life through the experience of 'voluntary'[29] work. As such it fell within the general category of individualized sentences to which most of the Advisory Council's proposals can be assigned. A difference was, however, that this reformative effect was to stem not from the imposition or choice of treatment or help, but from the provision of a different experience. Ken Pease[30] has pointed out many antecedents and analogies of community service in other judicial systems, and Bill McWilliams[31] has argued that the community service order is based on the assumption that the offender sentenced to it is 'moral ethical man', while probation 'treatment' is based on the idea that offenders receiving it are 'psychopathologically' or 'psychosocially' determined objects, with little or any free volition. For us, the moral tone of the community service order, as the Advisory Council saw it, seems analogous to the Benthamite notion of rehabilitation by meditation; certainly, however, despite the similarity of its objectives to those of the treatment model (and the indirectness of the process by which rehabilitation is achieved),[32] the proposal of community service had the unusual characteristic that the offender was expected to reform himself, rather than be reformed by another person's intervention.

The translation of the Council's recommendations into law was a complex process, and has been well documented elsewhere.[33] The Advisory Council's recommendations were studied and amended by a working group set up by the Home Office. The working group's recommendations were incorporated with some changes into the 1972 Criminal Justice Bill. This contained provisions for the introduction of community service for offences that could otherwise have been punished by imprisonment. Community service would be for up to 240 hours under a new community service order (not a community service condition to a probation order as the Advisory Council had suggested). Community service orders could also be imposed for fine default and breach of probation (these two powers have not yet been implemented, although it seems likely that community service will soon be available as a sentence for fine defaulters); a breach of the order could be punished by a fine with the order allowed to continue; and community service schemes would be administered by the probation service.

It should be noted here that throughout the discussion of community service prior to its introduction, the Advisory Council, the Home Office Working Group and Parliament had all seen the probation service, because of its position in the criminal justice system, and its network of locally based offices, as being the appropriate agency to administer community service orders.

Following the passing of the 1972 Criminal Justice Act, 'experimental' community service schemes were set up in six probation areas (Inner London, Nottinghamshire, Shropshire, SW Lancashire, County Durham and Kent – the listing is in the order in which orders were made) early in 1973. The Home Office Research Unit was given the task of studying the introduction of community service in the six experimental areas, presumably in order that the Home Office could be advised about the viability of the new sentence and so that the lessons learnt in the experiments could be incorporated into newer schemes. In fact the Research Unit produced two reports on the experiments,[34] one in 1975 and one in 1977. There was a wealth of material, some descriptive and some evaluative, available to probation committees wishing to introduce community service schemes and, in addition, the Home Office made special funding available in 1978 to allow all areas to have a scheme. By early in 1979, schemes were in operation in all the 56 probation areas in England and Wales.

Thus the transition from experimental to national scheme was very fast and may well have produced wide, if not unacceptable, variations in the position of community service as a sentence.[35] It is not our purpose to deal with these variations, but to discuss in more general terms the role of the community service order as an alternative to custody.

Basically the community service order is a sentence of the court in which an offender undertakes to spend a set number of hours (varying from 40 to 240) doing unpaid work (generally, but not always, of the kind that is called 'voluntary') within a period of a year. The offender has to consent to the order being made and its terms are explained to him. A community service order can be made only in respect of an offence punishable by a custodial sentence. A breach of the terms of the order can be dealt with by the court by imposing another sentence (including imprisonment), by terminating the order, or by allowing it to continue. In general the procedures associated with community service orders are in law very similar to those associated with probation orders – the consent of the offender, breach proceedings – on which they were presumably modelled, but there are significant differences in practice (the decision to take breach proceedings, for example)[36] and one particular one in law: if no one takes any action, the order can continue indefinitely until the work is done (unlike a probation order which expires automatically on a set date unless it is terminated earlier).[37]

As the compilers of the Home Office *Probation and After-Care Statistics* for 1980 say, 'Whether a community service order should be seen solely as an alternative to imprisonment or as a sentence in its own right has been the subject of discussion since the inception of the scheme.'[38] At the beginning of the scheme, this discussion appears to have been complicated by the question of how community service might work for offenders. The Advisory Council's report had argued that community service would help to reform offenders by giving them alternative experiences of life – working in a children's home instead of stealing cars, to take a fictional example. In many of the early reports on community service a kind of mythology of rehabilitation was built up around such cases, and especially those where the ex-offender continued his or her community work after the order had expired.[39] This mythology was (like all mythologies) based on truth and indeed there were, and continue to be, many cases where an offender has taken up voluntary work and/or apparently ceased offending as a result of his or her experiences of community service; similarly there are many cases where the influence, advice, help or treatment of a probation officer in a probation order is sufficient to change an offender's life. It must also be said that the mythology served a purpose in helping community service to gain wider acceptance through publicity than it might otherwise have done.

More sober reflection, however, suggests that these rehabilitative successes have not been so frequent as was implied; many work placements are of necessity unglamorous, isolated, and do little to give an offender an alternative view of the world, and it is perhaps for this reason that when the Home Office Research Unit looked at the reconviction rates of early community service orders they found them to be as high (or as low) as those of equivalent offenders given other sentences.[40]

There is no reason to believe that this position has changed substantially in the last six or seven years. About three-quarters of community service orders terminating do so because the offender has completed his or her hours; about one in ten are breached for reoffending during the order and about one in seven or eight for not complying with the order. In addition, some orders cannot be terminated because clients have disappeared and warrants are out for their arrests. These figures, which reflect wide variations over England and Wales, do not appear to be substantially different from those recorded by the six experimental areas in the early years of the scheme.[41]

In 1982 nearly 31,000 offenders received community service orders and most of these (28,000) were as sentences for indictable offences – 7 per cent of the total number sentenced aged 17 or over. This figure represented a 10 per cent increase over the number given community service in 1981 (28,000) and a 96 per cent increase over the number in 1979 (16,000). While community service is used relatively more often for younger offenders, its recent rate of growth has been higher in the sentencing of those aged over twenty (who in 1982 accounted for over half of the orders made).[42] The indications are that these trends are continuing, although the availability of work to be done, and of resources to supervise it, may impose limits to growth.[43] In Inner London, for example, the rapid expansion of the scheme in its early years reached a temporary plateau in the late 1970s from which only the 'explosion' of sentences in 1980 removed it.

There is no doubt then that the community service order is an increasingly popular sentence with the courts. As it becomes more frequently used, however, so its status in the tariff, and particularly its role as an alternative to custody, come more under judicial scrutiny. Although the Advisory Council perceived community service as applicable to a wide range of offences, the Home Office Working Party, together with the Governments which successively set up the new sentence and expanded its use, saw it primarily, if not wholly, as an alternative to prison. The 1972 Criminal Justice Act itself referred to community service orders being made in cases where the offence could be dealt with by a custodial sentence, but did not specifically say that they could be made only when the court would otherwise have sent the offender to prison, detention centre or borstal. Nevertheless, it was the latter interpretation that successive Home Office ministers endorsed and promoted whenever the need or occasion arose.[44] Similarly, three of the six experimental probation areas used, or attempted to use, their community service schemes as alternatives to custody.[45]

The fact is that the policies and practices of these three areas, and the statements of Home Office ministers, went some way beyond the letter (if not the spirit) of the Act. (It may be that the ministers' statements encapsulated their Governments' *intentions* with regard to the use of community service, even if the wording of the Act demonstrated an inability or unwillingness to make these explicit.) They also went beyond a consensus, even in the original six experimental areas, as to the purpose of community service – in three areas it was *not* seen as an alternative to custody – and perhaps also beyond the views and practices of judges and magistrates in this matter.

The assessment of community service orders carried out in 1976 by the Home Office Research Unit attempted, among other things, to estimate how far they *were* being used as an alternative to custody.[46] Lacking evidence from 'controlled experiments' (i.e. where offenders were randomly assigned to courts that could make community service orders or to courts that could not) or from detailed comparative studies between the experimental areas and others, the researchers were forced to use indirect ways of estimating how far community service diverted offenders from custody. These were, briefly:

assessment by the probation officer writing the social inquiry report as to the risk of an immediate custodial sentence if the order were not made;

monitoring sentences passed on offenders for whom a community service order was recommended but not made;

analysing the sentences passed on offenders who had breached their community service order and worked fewer than 10 per cent of the hours ordered;

analysing the sentences passed in cases where the courts had *requested* an assessment of suitability for community service but had not made such an order (the courts do not always take the initiative in suggesting community service).

The first three methods all produced estimates that around 50 per cent of community service orders were being made instead of immediate custodial sentences. The last method indicated that only about one order in five was an alternative to custody.

The team of Home Office researchers took this last and atypical figure as showing the real position of community service, although the chief author of their report, Ken Pease, has since written that he finds the estimate of about 50 per cent (derived from the other three methods of estimation) more persuasive.[47] Even this, however, makes community service only about as effective an alternative as the suspended sentence has been and, like the suspended sentence, the community service order carries with it the risk that an offender can be sent to prison for breaking the conditions of an order imposed when he or she was *not* at risk of a custodial sentence for the original offence. Indeed, the less effective community service is as a non-custodial alternative, the greater the risk of unjust custodial sentences in following breach proceedings. It is also noteworthy that the figures presented by the researchers suggest that probation areas' individual policies on the role of community service had little or no discernible effect on local courts' use of it as an alternative to custody.

Despite this, the popularity of community service with the courts needs some explaining. Part of the reason may be the speed with which the Home Office allowed the scheme to be expanded (by contrast with day training centres, which have never expanded beyond their four original areas), and this in turn may well be related to the fact that community service schemes were to be funded on the same basis as most probation service work – 80 per cent from the Government and 20 per cent from the local authority (whereas day training centres were funded 100 per cent by the Government). A second reason is that the managements of probation services promoted the scheme enthusiastically at a time when the perceived failure of the IMPACT experiment and Martinson's view that 'nothing works' appeared, as we have seen, to have shaken their confidence in the probation order as an effective sentence. (It is fair to say, however, that the National Association of Probation Officers has been less enamoured of community service; they opposed its operation by the probation service and have always been concerned, with some justice, that its introduction contributed to the decline of the probation order.)

Chief Probation Officers' enthusiasm for community service orders was probably heightened by the fact that they appear to be relatively cheap to administer. In 1980 community service orders comprised about a ninth of the probation service's total caseload, but only 3 per cent of the service's 'professional' manpower (i.e. including probation officers, seniors, chief officer grades, but excluding ancillary workers and administrative staff) worked in community service schemes, which were substantially staffed by ancillary workers – paid less than probation officers and, in some areas at least, considered more appropriate as supervisors of community service orders.[48]

In reality the difference in costs between community service and probation may be less than these figures suggest. The Home Office has estimated that at 1981–2 prices it cost on average £520 to supervise an offender on probation for one year, and £490 to supervise an offender on community service for the same period. As the average community service order is terminated within about eight months, however, the cost of each order may be only two-thirds of that figure: about £330.[49]

Nevertheless, neither the enthusiasm of the Home Office nor that of the Chief Probation Officers can explain the rapidity with which the courts turned to community service as a sentencing option. The perceived low cost of the order may have played a part, but a better explanation may be the diverse moral appeal of community service, its capacity to be, as Maurice Vanstone and Peter Raynor put it, 'all things to all men'.[50] For community service, conceived in the autumn of the treatment ideal, has the capacity to be represented as meeting needs for 'treatment', for punishment, for reparation and for the enlightenment of the offender.

It is true that at least some of the experimental areas attempted to distance community service from probation as a form of treatment. For example, the Inner London Probation and After-Care Service, in its booklet *ILPAS '76* (commemorating the 'centenary' of probation in London), said:

> The experience of Inner London in the first three years has indicated that a community service order is not the answer for people who have problems of addiction or are in need of skilled casework help.[51]

but it also claimed that the community service order 'encompasses the concepts both of retribution and rehabilitation'[52] and that those supervising offenders on community service could, 'through positive interaction with the offenders . . . often initiate constructive changes in attitudes and behaviour'.[53] Ken Pease, in his brief history of community service, comments that Inner London, in developing and setting up its scheme, had 'stressed community service as an alternative to custody perhaps more clearly and consistently than any other of the [experimental] areas'.[54] Other areas apparently laid greater stress on the therapeutic benefits of community service; Bill McWilliams quotes the South Yorkshire County Co-Ordinator as suggesting that probation officers consider for community service not only those liable to a custodial sentence but also 'any offenders an officer feels would benefit from the experience'.[55]

Such evidence as there is, however, suggests that probation services attempted to maintain a distinction of kind as well as degree between community service and probation orders, even if this was made less clear through references to the good effects of community service on offenders. Such references have perhaps served to disguise the onerousness of a community service order.

In 1982, two out of every five offenders receiving community service orders had to work between 100 and 150 hours, and the average total order length was probably about 150 hours overall. Orders of this length were usually completed in seven or eight months, an average of 20 hours' work each month, four or five hours' work each week. About one offender in five had to serve an order of 200 hours or more, and these were usually completed in about nine months – 22 hours' work a month.[56] Given that these orders were expected to be completed in an offender's spare time (although, with the growth in unemployment levels, this is an increasingly redundant concept), they demand a level of sustained commitment higher than most people are prepared to give to their hobbies, sports or voluntary activities.

This point has now been recognized by the courts. In the case *Regina v Lawrence* in 1982 the Court of Appeal commented that short community service orders were equivalent to other non-custodial sentences; longer orders, however, should be seen as equating to prison sentences, and the court suggested that an order of 190 hours should be regarded as on a level with a twelve-month prison sentence.[57]

Similarly, His Honour Judge Goldstone, writing in *The Magistrate*,[58] suggested a tariff for community service orders based on three principles:

> that 5 hours of community service were approximately equal to one day's work;

that 20 hours should take a month to complete;

that 4 hours were the equivalent of a £6 fine.

The tariff he devised was as follows:

Hours of Community Service	*Amount of Fine*	*Length of Custodial Sentence*
40	£60	
80	£120	14 days
100	£150	1 month
140	£260	6 months
200	£300	9 months
240	£1,000	over 12 months

While Judge Goldstone's proposed tariff is not exactly the same as that suggested by the Appeal Court's comments, it is nevertheless of the same order of magnitude.

These recent judicial views of community service accord well with the philosophy that Ken Pease has pursued ever since he left the Home Office Research Unit, of community service being used as a *sentence in its own right*. In his latest publication[59] Dr Pease has built on earlier proposals of his to set a tariff for community service – based on the proposition that only orders of 100 hours or over should be substitutes for prison sentences, on the basis of each 30 hours over 100 being equal to a three-month prison sentence – and has also suggested that community service should be used instead of fines, which defendants are often unable to pay.

An editorial in the periodical *Justice of the Peace*, welcoming these ideas and pointing to the relevance of the *Regina v Lawrence* decision, queried (for reasons that are unclear to us) the value of a tariff for community service as precise as those we have been discussing, but observed with some justice that on any basis (if the Court of Appeal's valuation is even reasonably accurate) many magistrates' courts (which have powers only to impose a six-month prison sentence) are making community service orders that are too long.[60]

One conclusion from this is that they have been doing so precisely because community service has lacked in the past the uncontested status of being a sentence in its own right. Its presentation as an alternative to custody, linked often with emphases on its beneficial effects on offenders, may well have encouraged courts to sentence offenders more severely than they deserve – the classic criticism of the 'treatment model' of sentencing.

Paradoxically, therefore, it may be that community service will become more effective as an alternative to imprisonment as it continues to lose its special 'alternative' status and becomes increasingly accepted as a sentence in its own right.

NOTES AND REFERENCES

1 The figures given here are taken from statistics presented in D. Haxby, *Probation, a Changing Service*, London: Constable, 1978, table 21, p. 152.

2 Home Office, *Criminal Statistics, England and Wales 1981*, London: HMSO, 1982.

3 See G.J.O. Philpotts and L.B. Lancucki, *Previous Convictions, Sentence and Reconviction*, Home Office Research Study No. 53, London: HMSO, 1979. Walker's (1981) argument, quoted in Chapter 4, that different sentences for similar offences do have differential reconviction rates for different risk groups, does not affect this point – that, *overall*, suspended sentences appear to be no more effective than any other disposal at preventing further reconviction. It may well be that there are kinds of offenders for whom suspended sentences are particularly effective, but, if so, they have not yet been identified.

4 Ibid.

5 R.F. Sparks, 'The Use of Suspended Sentences', *Criminal Law Review*, 1971, pp. 384–401.

6 See E. Oatham and F. Simon, 'Are Suspended Sentences Working?', *New Society*, 3 August, 1972, pp. 233–5.

7 See K. Pease, 'Community Service and Prison: Are They Alternatives?', in K. Pease and W. McWilliams (eds), *Community Service by Order*, Edinburgh: Scottish Academic Press, 1980, pp. 38 and 39, and R.F. Sparks, 'The Use of Suspended Sentences', op. cit.

8 The measure of closeness to fines and probation depends on what proportion of suspended sentences would have been replaced by these two disposals. The evidence we quote suggests more than half; nobody seems to be suggesting significantly less than half. The position of probation as slightly outside the tariff makes this argument more complex, but does not invalidate it. Probation, as a court disposal chosen, it is argued, on the basis of need rather than just deserts, substitutes for and is substituted by a variety of sentences, including suspended sentences. In any case, the evidence is, we suggest, that probation is moving closer to the tariff.

9 House of Commons Fifteenth Report from the Expenditure Committee, Session 1977–1978, *The Reduction of Pressure on the Prison System*, Vol. I, London: HMSO, 1978.

10 Home Office, *Review of Parole*, London: Home Office, 1981.

11 Reported in *Justice of the Peace*, 6 May, 1982; *Daily Telegraph*, 8 February, 1982; and *NACRO Briefing: The Partly Suspended Sentence*, November 1981.

12 *NACRO Briefing*, op. cit.

13 Reported in the *Daily Telegraph*, 8 February, 1982.

14 Advisory Council on the Penal System, *Sentences of Imprisonment: A Review of Maximum Penalties*, London: HMSO, 1978.

15 Ibid.

16 Advisory Council on the Penal System, *Report on Non-Custodial and Semi-Custodial Penalties*, London: HMSO, 1970.

17 G. Wilkins, *Making Them Pay: A Study of Some Fine-Defaulters, Civil Prisoners and Other Petty Offenders in a Local Prison*, London: NACRO, 1979.

18 W. Miles, 'Fine Default by Persons under Twenty-One Years of Age', *Justice of the Peace*, Vol. 147, No. 41, 1983, pp. 643–5.

19 G. Wilkins, *Making Them Pay*, op. cit.

20 P. Softley, 'The Imprisonment of Fine Defaulters, *Justice of the Peace*, Vol. 147, No. 30, 1983, pp. 470–72.

21 Ibid. These estimates of ability to pay suffer from the fact that sufficient information to make them was lacking in a third of the cases studied.

22 G. Wilkins, *Making Them Pay*, op. cit.

23 See Chapter 4.

24 Home Office, *Probation Statistics, England and Wales 1982*, London: Home Office, 1984.

25 Ibid.

26 Ibid.

27 Ibid.

28 Advisory Council on the Penal System, *Report on Non-Custodial and Semi-Custodial Penalties*, op. cit.

29 Offenders on community service orders are not 'volunteers', but the work they do is generally of the kind that would otherwise be done by volunteers.

30 K. Pease, 'A Brief History of Community Service', in K. Pease and W. McWilliams (eds), *Community Service by Order*, Edinburgh: Scottish Academic Press, 1980, pp. 1–13.

31 W. McWilliams, 'Models of Man and Community Service', in K. Pease and W. McWilliams (eds), *Community Service by Order*, op. cit., pp. 14–26.

32 One aspect of the 'treatment' approach was that the client's overt wishes were to be seen only as symptoms of a deeper malaise. But because this malaise was deep-seated, it could only be treated indirectly 'by stealth'.

33 For a description of the process by which the Advisory Council's recommendation was turned into law see K. Pease, 'A Brief History of Community Service', op. cit.

34 K. Pease *et al.*, *Community Service Orders*, Home Office Research Study No. 29, London: HMSO, 1975, and K. Pease *et al.*, *Community Service Assessed in 1976*, Home Office Research Study No. 39, London: HMSO, 1977.

35 See K. Pease, 'Community Service and Prison: Are They Alternatives?', op. cit.

36 See W. McWilliams and N. Murphy, 'Breach of Community Service', in K. Pease and W. McWilliams (eds), *Community Service by Order*, op. cit.

37 In practice, community service orders which have remained current for more than two years are often terminated or rescinded by agreement with magistrates.

38 Home Office, *Probation and After-Care Statistics, England and Wales 1980*, London: Home Office, 1981, p. 40.

39 See *ILPAS '76: A Report on Aspects of the Work of the Inner London Probation and After-Care Service*, London: ILPAS, 1976, p. 50.

40 K. Pease *et al.*, *Community Service Assessed in 1976*, op. cit.

41 See, for example, *ILPAS '76*, op. cit., in comparison with Home Office, *Probation Statistics, England and Wales 1982*, op. cit.

42 Home Office, *Probation Statistics, England and Wales 1982*, op. cit.

43 Ibid.

44 See K. Pease, 'Community Service and Prison: Are They Alternatives?', op. cit., pp. 29, 35 and 36.

45 Ibid.

46 K. Pease *et al., Community Service Assessed in 1976*, op. cit.

47 K. Pease, 'Community Service and Prison: Are They Alternatives?', op. cit., p. 35.

48 See Home Office, *Probation Statistics, England and Wales 1982*, op. cit., Chapter 10, pp. 82–7, for the relative employment of probation officers and ancillaries in community service schemes.

49 This figure is calculated from those quoted in the *Probation Statistics, England and Wales 1982*, op. cit., p. 102.

50 M. Vanstone and P. Raynor, 'Diversion from Prison – Partial Success and a Missed Opportunity', *Probation Journal*, Vol. 28, No. 3, 1981, pp. 85–9.

51 *ILPAS '76*, op. cit., p. 50.

52 Ibid.

53 Ibid.

54 K. Pease, 'A Brief History of Community Service', op. cit., pp. 11–12.

55 W. McWilliams, 'Selection Policies for Community Service', in K. Pease and W. McWilliams (eds), *Community Service by Order*, op. cit., p. 45.

56 See Home Office, *Probation Statistics, England and Wales 1982*, op. cit., Chapter 6. The number of hours' work a month required to complete an order is estimated from the published statistics.

57 'Notes of the Week', *Justice of the Peace*, Vol. 146, No. 30, 1982, pp. 443–4.

58 His Honour Judge Goldstone, 'A Fresh Look at Community Service Orders', *The Magistrate*, May 1982.

59 K. Pease, *Community Service Orders: A First Decade of Promise*, London: Howard League for Penal Reform, 1982.

60 'Notes of the Week', *Justice of the Peace*, op. cit.

Chapter Six

EMPTYING THE PRISONS

One weapon that Governments have at their disposal when faced with an over-large prison population is to exercise an apparent vestige of the old royal prerogative of mercy and arrange for prisoners to be released before they have served the full terms of their sentences. Thus, in the mid-1920s, the Conservative Home Secretary, Winston Churchill, achieved an arbitrary (but successful) reduction in sentence lengths of one-half, releasing from prison all those who had served more than 50 per cent of their original sentence. Such decisive strokes are, by their very nature, rare, but in more recent years measures have been adopted which have as their basic assumption that prisoners should be kept in prison for less time than judges' sentences say they should.

These measures are remission of sentence (for good behaviour) and parole. Taken together they might suggest to a layman that the executive branch of Government believes that the prison sentences handed down by the judiciary are generally too severe, but feels unable to deal with this problem directly by changing the laws relating to sentencing, and so has to resort to covert measures instead. Against this is the fact that the 'rules' governing remission and parole are well known to the judiciary, who themselves have some freedom to adjust their sentencing practices accordingly.

Remission and parole are in fact two very different procedures, adopted for different reasons, but they are connected, as we shall see, in their operations and effects and so merit being discussed together here.

Remission means that any prisoner serving a determinate (i.e. fixed) sentence of over six months can have the final third remitted (set aside) if he or she behaves well while in prison. In other words, prisoners sentenced to twelve months need only spend eight months inside, provided they behave themselves. The remission system has obvious value as an aid to prison discipline, providing an incentive to prisoners to co-operate with the prison regime, and as a weapon by which governors can discipline those who do not. Whether remission acts by itself to keep the prison population from rising further, or whether judges have adjusted to it and now sentence on the time they expect the prisoner to serve, is unclear. On balance the latter seems the more likely; in which case loss of remission becomes in effect an additional punishment imposed for deviant behaviour *in prison*.

While remission is the right of every medium or long-term prisoner until he or she loses it, parole is a self-confessed privilege to be earned by a selected minority. Originally, in the seventeenth century, the term 'parole' meant in English a legal undertaking or promise. It was also used specifically to refer to promises given by released prisoners-of-war (usually officers) not to fight again in a particular conflict, and this may be one of the antecedents of its modern usage to indicate release from prison under some form of licence.

Parole was first introduced to England and Wales by the 1967 Criminal Justice Act, whose provisions were based on the 1965 report of the Advisory Council, *The Adult Offender*. Parole systems had already been operating in many other jurisdictions, especially in the USA, for many years with some evident success. Indeed the idea of parole had been foreshadowed over a century earlier within the United Kingdom by the use of 'tickets of leave' as an element in an offender's progression through a structured prison system from regulated confinement to complete freedom. This experiment by Sir Walter Crofton, Chairman of the Board of Directors of Irish Prisons, left little impression on English penological thinking, however, perhaps because of the restrictive effects of the ticket-of-leave system in England.

While parole is often associated with the treatment ideology, and was especially used in America as the reward for co-operation with the supposed therapy of a prison sentence, *The Adult Offender* report was rather more modest in its thinking. Its argument for parole was in essence that for some prisoners the benefits (to society) of their serving a full sentence were outweighed by the harmful effects (on them) of so doing.

A connection with the treatment ideology was made during the parliamentary debates on the parole proposals contained in the 1967 Criminal Justice Bill when the then Home Secretary, Roy Jenkins, spoke of prisoners attaining 'a peak of training'[1] during their sentences, at which they would benefit most from an early release. (Latterly the argument has been put another way, with the suggestion that early release on parole helps to mitigate the failure of prisons to provide effective treatment.)

In fact, most of the parliamentary debate about parole in 1967 focused not on the desirability or otherwise of such a measure, but on the way the scheme should operate. The original proposal contained in the Bill was that cases of prisoners eligible for parole should be reviewed by informal committees within the prisons; these committees would make recommendations to the Home Secretary who would then decide whether or not to grant parole in each individual case. This process was amended, on the basis of proposals by the Conservative opposition, to include an independent body, the Parole Board (as it came to be called), which would make a final recommendation to the Home Secretary for or against parole.

Following the passing of the 1967 Criminal Justice Act, the Parole Board was set up under the Chairmanship of Lord Hunt. As originally constituted, the decision-making process for parole was as follows:

1. A committee based on each prison (known as the Local Review Committee and including representatives of the judiciary or magistrates and the probation service) scrutinized each parole application. (Prisoners eligible for parole have to apply for it.)
2. In each case the Local Review Committee sent a recommendation, for or against parole, to the Home Secretary.
3. The Home Secretary forwarded those cases he accepted as being suitable for parole to the Parole Board.
4. The Parole Board made a recommendation for or against parole.
5. The Home Secretary could overrule the Parole Board's recommendation for parole (although this rarely happens).
6. Cases where parole had been refused were reviewed again every twelve months (or sooner if the prisoner was coming to the end of his sentence).

Two modifications were subsequently made to this system. From the end of 1969 cases forwarded to the Parole Board included as a matter of course all those whose parole application had been rejected by the Local Review Committee (LRC), but who appeared, on statistical grounds, to be unlikely to reoffend within two years of their release. According to the Home Office *Review of Parole*, this had the objective of evening out Local Review Committees' decisions, so that prisoners' chances of parole were not unduly affected by the prison they were at and the context in which their case was seen. Second, the Criminal Justice Act 1972 (Section 35) empowered the Home Secretary to release some types of prisoners on parole if this was recommended by the Local Review Committee, without referring their case to the Parole Board. The criteria for applying this power have twice been widened (in 1974 and 1976) and now cover all prisoners sentenced to two years or less, and those sentenced to four years or less if they have not been imprisoned for offences involving sex, violence, arson or drug trafficking. Further, in 1975, the Home Secretary produced a new set of guidelines on suitability for parole, with the objective of persuading the Local Review Committees and the Parole Board to be less conservative in their recommendations and decisions, and to release more prisoners on parole.

The net result of these changes was that parole was granted nearly twice as often in 1979 as in 1969: in 1979 44 per cent of those eligible for parole (47 per cent of those applying) received it, as Chart 1 shows, compared with 25 per cent of those eligible in 1969 (see Chart 2).[2]

The chart shows that two-fifths of those paroled in 1979 were granted parole by the Home Secretary under the 1972 Criminal Justice Act as a result of Local Review Committees' recommendations. Nearly two-thirds of those recommended for parole by Local

CHART 1

The Parole Process 1979

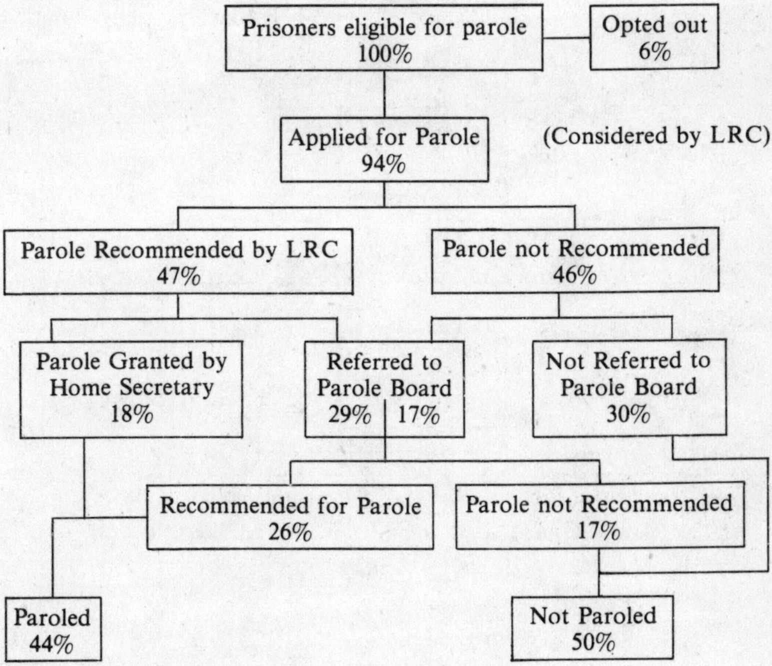

Review Committees, however, were referred to the Parole Board, which also considered over a third of those cases rejected by the Committees. The Parole Board itself recommended parole in just over half the cases it considered, rejecting some of the Committee's recommendations, and accepted some of the cases that the Committees had rejected.

As a comparison of Chart 1 with Chart 2[3] shows, the main change in the decade 1969–79 has been in the role of the Local Review Committees, which have become both more influential and more 'adventurous' in their recommendations. Whereas in 1969 the Committees recommended parole less than one time in three, ten years later they did so in every other case they considered. The main causes of this change are probably to be found in the revised parole guidelines issued by the Home Secretary in 1975; while the Committees had been recommending parole more frequently every

CHART 2

The Parole Process 1969

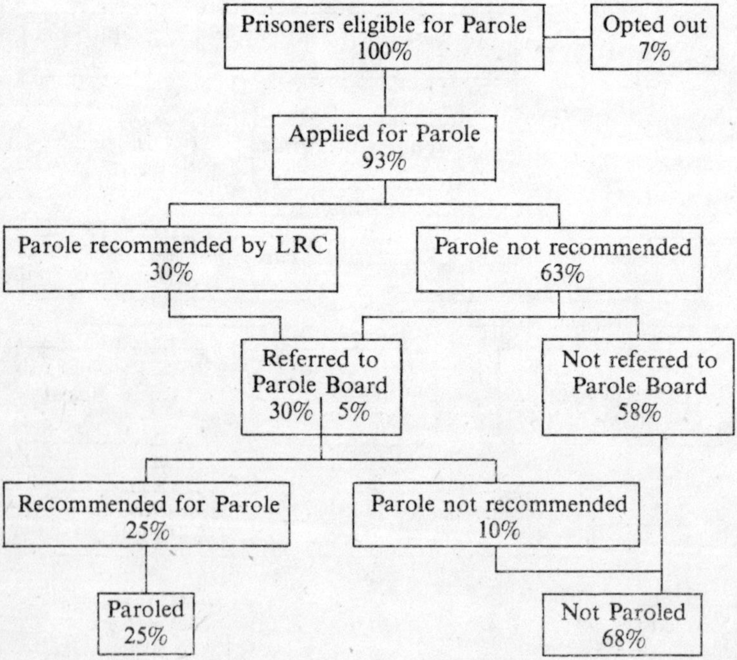

year, the biggest jump in the recommendation rate was the increase from 41 per cent in 1975 to 48 per cent in 1976, the year after the new guidelines had been issued.

A second trend has been for the Parole Board to look at more cases which have not been recommended for parole by the Local Review Committees. In 1969 only 8 per cent of such cases were considered by the Board; this proportion rose to 19 per cent the following year, to 22 per cent in 1973, to 30 per cent in 1974 and to 35 per cent in 1978. These changes do not appear to be related to developments in Local Review Committees' decision making, nor to the 1975 guidelines, but are probably due to developments in the identification of potential parolees through statistical prediction methods. It must be pointed out, however, that the Parole Board appears considerably *less* likely to recommend parole in these cases than it is in cases referred positively from Local Review Committees. Thus, in 1979, whereas the Board recommended parole in three out of five cases where a Local Committee had done so, the same result occurred in only one out of every four cases when the Committee had not recommended parole. Indeed less than 10 per cent of the grants of parole were made in respect of cases which the Local Review Committee had considered unsuitable.

Thus a prisoner's chances of getting parole depend on the decisions of three very different kinds of body: the Local Review Committee, the Parole Board, and the Parole Unit at the Home Office (which, among other duties, advises the Home Secretary on Section 35 grants of parole). Of these, the Local Review Committee appears the most powerful, in that very few prisoners it views as unsuitable get parole, but a majority of those it thinks are suitable do get parole. The roles of the Board and the Parole Unit appear to be to act as checks on the Review Committees, to select out cases the latter have recommended rather than to select in ones they have rejected. It may be, however, that this itself makes Committees more ready to recommend parole than they would otherwise have been.

The problem with the parole system is that although it achieves the early release of nearly 5,000 prisoners a year, the way it does so appears arbitrary and unjust. One must also add that about one in six of these (approximately 800 prisoners) are paroled less than three months before their sentences are due to end; some of them must wonder whether their early release was worth their involvement in the system itself.

The main criticisms that have been levelled at the parole system have two components. The first is that, because decisions about parole are taken in secret, and because parolees are not told the reasons why their applications are rejected, the decision-making process is arbitrary and this arbitrariness leads to injustices. The second element is the criticism that the parole system is based on ideas of rehabilitation and treatment which are demonstrably inappropriate and unworkable now (if they ever were) in Britain's 'penal dustbins'. These two critiques come together in the general 'justice' critique, that we have already encountered, of the sentencing and treatment (in the non-therapeutic sense) of offenders.

Basically this critique sees parole as a denial of justice because parole decisions seem to be based not on what the offender has done to merit punishment, but on the way he has responded to the regime of the prison where he is serving his sentence. Its exponents deny the validity of ideas such as a 'peak of treatment' and argue that as parole is a part of a false and discredited ideology of treatment, it serves, along with other manifestations of the ideology, to keep people in prison for longer than justice requires. Thus parole, far from emptying the prisons, helps to support the system that keeps them full. The abolition of parole, therefore, would be a step towards shorter sentences based only on the just deserts merited by each offence.

This is a very powerful argument, put forward by some of the leading critics of our penal system. The problem is that, as with monetarism, the justice model does not work.

Many American states – following the argument (or a variant of it) set out above – have abolished parole and significantly reduced judges' discretion in dealing with offenders by imposing sentencing guidelines or mandatory sentences. The result, almost invariably, has been to *increase* the numbers of offenders sent to prison.

It is true that some of the reasons for this failure of the justice model lie in the peculiarities of the American legal system. For example, in American law, it is not possible to appeal against sentence, only against conviction. This means that the kind of moderating effect that the Court of Appeal can exercise over English and Welsh judges can be achieved in America only by administrative reviews within the parole system.[4]

A second consideration is that justice depends on sentencing for the *offence*. Unfortunately, the practice in America of bargaining between the defence and prosecution lawyers to arrive at a charge to which the defendant will plead guilty (thus sparing the State the expense of a jury trial) means that many defendants are sentenced on indictments that bear little relationship to the offence they are supposed to have committed. In this situation the exact nature and status of the offence for which sentence is being passed becomes unclear.[5]

Finally, if discretion is removed from judges' sentencing and from decision-making about the length of time in custody after sentence, it appears not to be destroyed but to be vested elsewhere. In American jurisdictions a large part of that discretion has reverted, as it were, to the legislatures, who often, at a time when crime appears to be on the increase, fall prey to temptations to make sentencing laws or guidelines even more draconian than they already are.

The net effect of these tendencies has been to make American prisons even more overcrowded than before in those very areas where parole has been abolished or its effects much reduced.[6]

If we accept then that the justice critique of parole has some limitations, we still need not agree that our present system is perfect. What research there has been into the British parole system has shown its main defects and injustices to be its secrecy and arbitrariness. The parole system is arbitrary because its decision-making is hidden, because the ideas underpinning the system, such as 'a peak of treatment' or its analogues, are difficult to apply consistently or justly, have indeed only dubious validity and may be only tenuously related to the reasons why the offender is in prison. Finally, because the system is decentralized, it is probable (despite the Home Office's efforts to pick equally 'good risks' from among those rejected by LRCs) that an offender's chances of getting parole depend as much on where he is (and thus on whom he is competing with) as they do on the strengths or weaknesses of his case.

Most parole applicants dislike the secrecy of the system, the fact that they know little of the way in which they will be assessed, or of the information on which the assessment will be based, and especially that they know nothing of the reasons behind the recommendations and decisions of the LRC and Parole Board. This is important because, among the feelings with which parolees leave prison is a sense of the injustice of the process which led to their release, and such a feeling can hardly contribute to their (re)adjustment to the values of 'straight' society.

None of these criticisms is particularly new, and most of them, particularly that of secrecy, have been levelled at parole since its inception. Although the Home Office has tended, as in its *Review of Parole*,[7] to deny their validity or the possibility of their being met, the Howard League has recently produced some worthy proposals for reforming the parole system. These are set out in its book *Freedom on Licence* (1981)[8] in which the main proposals are:

a) automatic release on licence after serving one-third of the sentence for those sentenced to seven years or less, with the proviso that for sentences of over three years the court would be able, if it wished, to specify a minimum time served in custody (over one-third of the sentence) before release on licence;

b) parole review, as at present, for those sentenced to over seven years (after one-third had been served);

c) the right of rejected parole applicants to appeal against Parole Board decisions to a 'Parole Division' of the Court of Appeal – in these cases the Home Secretary would have to show why the prisoner could not be released;

d) supervision of parolees (usually by probation officers) for up to the two-thirds point in their sentence, but with the supervisory conditions able to be suspended on application to the Parole Board;

e) abolition of Local Review Committees;

f) review of life sentence prisoners for release after three years of the sentence has been served.

These proposals would, if implemented, have the effect of taking out of the parole system at least two-thirds of the prisoners currently dealt with by it and of releasing most of them at least as early, and more certainly, than parole would have done. The sentencing of medium-term prisoners would become more determinate than the parole system allows it to be, and the Parole Board's decisions would become accountable to the courts and the judiciary.

Whether these changes would actually mean the release of more offenders from prison than the present system achieves is another matter. It is, for example, not impossible that judges would revise their sentencing decisions on the basis of what they expected an offender to serve, imposing longer sentences than they do at present.

There is a passing similarity between the Howard League's proposals and the expedient put forward in the Home Office *Review of Parole* of supervised release, after one-third of the sentence had been served, of those whose prison sentences were too short for parole. Both proposed automatic release for those who fell outside the limits of the parole system, although they made very different assumptions about the nature of that system. The Home Office estimated that its proposals would result in the immediate release of some 7,000 prisoners – possibly an overestimate.[9]

The Home Office proposal received a mixed welcome in the various parts of the criminal justice system and the agencies associated with it. It was welcomed on the grounds that it would reduce the prison population, but criticized because it appeared to interfere retrospectively with judges' discretion in sentencing, and welcomed not entirely enthusiastically within the probation service because of doubts about the value of supervision by probation officers for the relatively short periods envisaged.

At what appeared to be the last minute, when he had been expected by some to announce the introduction of supervised release, William Whitelaw, the then Home Secretary, drew back from this and, in his speech to the 1981 Annual General Meeting of NACRO, announced instead his plans to introduce the partially suspended sentence to reduce the prison population. It was rumoured at the time that the Home Secretary had been persuaded to change his mind, and to reverse the apparent trend of Home Office policies, by the judges, who had refused to accept the idea of supervised release as it stood then. It is noteworthy, however, that the idea was incorporated into the 1982 Criminal Justice Act, with the proviso that the sentencing judge can (as the Howard League suggested in its proposals) specify the minimum time to be served in custody.

What is significant about this is not the alleged influence of the judiciary over the then Home Secretary (an influence he has always denied), but the fact that a new principle of sentencing seems to be emerging – that offenders sent to prison will serve only a short part of their notional sentence there, and a further part under some form of constraint (supervision by a probation officer; threat of another prison sentence) in the community.

Thus, although an opportunity was missed to free 7,000 prisoners, it may be that the outcome has laid the foundations for a more significant change in English and Welsh sentencing practice. It remains to be seen, however, whether and how Home Secretaries will use the opportunity given to them, and whether their doing so will lead to any reduction in the numbers in prison or sent there.

In all the discussions of parole and supervised remission one crucial element in the scheme tends to be ignored or dismissed. That is the supervision of parolees by probation officers. The tone was set by Morris and Beverley's study *On Licence*,[10] which commented on the apparent irrelevance and ineffectuality of probation officers in their role as supervisors of the licences. According to the Howard League,[11] the style and intensity of supervision is one of the key issues in the parole debate – even if it is hardly addressed in the proposals for reform. What then is this supervision?

In the 1960s the probation service acquired a general responsibility for helping ex-prisoners, and it already had a responsibility to *supervise* (on the assumption that their sentence was in some way therapeutic) young offenders discharged from prisons, borstals and detention centres, as well as some categories of adults from prisons and special hospitals.

The distinction between 'help' and 'supervision' is worth emphasizing here. 'Help' in this context means simply the provision of assistance to ex-prisoners on a voluntary, take-it-or-leave-it basis. This assistance could range from long-term casework to immediate aid with jobs, money or accommodation. 'Supervision', by contrast, implies that the probation officer is in some way responsible for controlling the behaviour of the offender and has sanctions, such as recall to custody, to use to this end and to enforce, however indirectly, the client's compliance with the supervision order or licence.

The distinction between the two had been blurred, partly because, as we have argued already, for probation officers the care/control dichotomy is an abstract rather than a practical one, and partly because this supervision was done within the 'treatment paradigm'. We have already observed that young offenders were given custodial sentences less frequently in the 1960s than they are in the 1980s, more or less irrespective of differences in offending patterns. In these circumstances it may have been easier to regard such sentences, and their subsequent periods of after-care, as being for offenders' benefit. (This is not meant to imply that probation officers recommended them to courts less thoughtfully or more often than they do now.) In addition, those who were being supervised in this way had often already been clients of the service.

Parolees, however were different. Although their release had been related to theoretical considerations of treatment, the supervising officer had probably been relatively uninvolved in these. Therefore the quasi-contractual nature of the relationship between supervisor and client that existed in a probation order, and might have existed in a borstal licence, for example, was probably conspicuous by its absence. Thus parole supervision was arguably different in content and purpose from the generality of probation work.

Morris and Beverley appear to have based their critique of supervision on the influential work of Mayer and Timms,[12] contrasting adversely the psychologically-influenced middle-class constructs of social workers with the practical needs of working-class clients. It will be apparent from our discussion of the probation order that this view has much of value in it, and latter-day versions of it appear in, for example, Beaumont and Walker's[13] critical analysis of the work of probation officers. It should also be apparent that this is not the whole truth of the matter. There has been a considerable amount of research[14] to suggest that clients' experiences of social work are not as negative, and not as bedevilled by misapprehensions, as these authors suggest.

Parole supervision is, on one level, a form of social work in that a part of the supervising officer's job is to help the parolee adjust to life on the outside, in both its practical and emotional aspects. To the extent that this work is successful it helps to remove or reduce material and personal incentives to reoffend; as a recent study in Inner London[15] suggests, probation officers can also protect their clients against over-enthusiastic attention from the police. All of these add up to a more positive value for parole supervision than Morris and Beverley suggested. What probation officers do not do is reinforce parolees' 'law-abiding behaviour' by *surveillance*, and it is in this area that their role has perhaps been misunderstood.

While the conditions of the parole licence, which are very like those of the probation order, help to provide grounds for deciding whether the licence has been breached or not, they offer very little to *ensure* that parolees do not reoffend. It is perfectly possible for a parolee to report to his probation officer, keep the conditions of his licence and still reoffend if he wishes. Nor, without knowledge that stems from the *casework relationship*, would the probation officer be able to avert this. It follows, therefore, that while there is a great deal that probation officers can do for and with parolees, there is little that they can do without them. If supervision and reporting on parole become merely routine surveillance, there is a good case, as the Howard League suggests, for removing the supervision requirement of a parole licence. While casework may only have a slight, if perhaps at times decisive, effect on whether a parolee reoffends, reporting alone will probably have none. There is evidence that when a parole supervision relationship does work it is because it has been established on the basic understanding of the positive role the probation officer can play in the parolee's readjustment to society. Parolees see the probation officer as an *ally* (or as neutral), not as an adversary.

To sum up: in general, parole, for all its faults, does take offenders out of prison and does demonstrate that even serious offenders can be supported in the community without undue risks. It is unlikely that the changes suggested or proposed to the system will affect this fact.

Postscript

Since this chapter was written the Home Secretary has introduced two changes into the parole system. The first change is that the threshold of parole eligibility has been dropped from twelve months to six, as the All-Party Penal Affairs Group had suggested. The second change is that, by contrast, life sentence prisoners convicted of certain kinds of murders will now normally serve at least twenty years in prison, while other violent offenders, and drug traffickers, will be expected to serve longer sentences before parole than they do at present.

NOTES AND REFERENCES

1 Quoted in Howard League for Penal Reform, *Freedom on Licence: The Development of Parole and Proposals for Reform*, Sunbury: Quartermaine House, 1981.

2 Based on statistics quoted in Home Office, *Review of Parole in England and Wales*, London: Home Office, 1981.

3 Ibid.

4 See Howard League for Penal Reform, *Freedom on Licence*, op. cit.

5 Ibid.

6 Ibid.

7 Home Office, *Review of Parole in England and Wales*, op. cit.

8 Howard League for Penal Reform, *Freedom on Licence*, op. cit.

9 Home Office, *Review of Parole in England and Wales*, op. cit.

10 P. Morris and F. Beverley, *On Licence: A Study of Parole*, London: John Wiley, 1972.

11 Howard League for Penal Reform, *Freedom on Licence*, op. cit.

12 J.E. Mayer and N. Timms, *The Client Speaks*, London: Routledge & Kegan Paul, 1970.

13 H. Walker and B. Beaumont, *Probation Work: Critical Theory and Socialist Practice*, Oxford: Basil Blackwell, 1981.

14 See, for example, the studies referred to in E.M. Goldberg, *Social Work since Seebohm: All Things to All Men?*, Eileen Younghusband Lecture, London: NISW, 1978.

15 J. Beazley, P. Maitland and P. O'Sullivan, *The Supervision of Parole*, London: ILPAS, 1982.

Chapter Seven

SPECIAL CASES

So far we have concentrated our discussion on alternatives to custodial sentences received as a result of a conviction for a criminal offence. It is generally recognized that the prisons in England and Wales hold many people who have not been convicted of a crime, and also many for whom the sanctions of criminal law are seen as poor substitutes for some other form of intervention, or for none at all. It is on these 'special cases' that we shall focus in this chapter.

They fall into two groups: the so-called 'unsentenced prisoners', and prisoners whose incarceration (and processing by the criminal justice system) is a fortuitous, if fated, outcome of behaviour which is only marginally, if at all, criminal in itself, resulting as it does from alcoholism, drug addiction or mental illness.

According to the Prison Department, about an eighth of its charges have not in fact been convicted of any crime.[1] The great majority of these are prisoners awaiting trial, on remand, or following committal for trial from a magistrates' court to the Crown Court. Each year roughly half a million people come before the courts charged with indictable offences. Over two-fifths of these are remanded by the magistrates' courts because their cases cannot be dealt with at one hearing or because the magistrates wish to have reports prepared on the defendant before passing sentence; most of these remands are at the instigation of the police, to allow them to prepare their evidence. About one in six of those who are remanded spend at least some time in custody – 40,000 extra prisoners in a year.

Of those appearing before magistrates' courts for indictable offences, about one in eight (74,000 in 1980) are not tried by magistrates, but committed to the Crown Court for trial by jury; about one in five of these (14,000 in 1980) are committed in custody. Finally, once the defendants reach the Crown Court, over a third of them (29,000 in 1980) are remanded in custody during their trial, for part of their trial, or between conviction and sentence.[2]

Obviously, many of those committed for trial, or remanded at the Crown Court in custody, will already have been remanded in custody by a magistrates' court, but one can probably not expect complete agreement between courts on when defendants should be remanded in custody or released on bail, and so it is probable that, in 1980 for example, the total number of defendants remanded in custody by the courts was somewhat larger than the 40,000 placed there by magistrates' courts. Despite the fact that some of these are remanded after conviction for medical or social inquiry reports, there is a substantial number of people charged with criminal offences who are put in custody but subsequently found to be innocent, and perhaps more who, after a remand in custody, are convicted but given a non-custodial sentence. The question is whether this use of prison by the courts can be reduced.

Remands are necessary for two reasons. The first is that, once a defendant has been brought before the courts, it is not always possible for the case to be tried immediately. The second is that judges and magistrates sometimes require medical and social inquiry reports before passing sentence.

The delays that occur in court proceedings stem partly from the busyness of the courts – so that each case, particularly when the defendant is pleading 'not guilty', has to take its place in the queue – and partly through the apparent need of the police to gather further evidence before starting their prosecution (or committal proceedings) in the magistrates' courts.

While the majority of defendants remanded at the courts are remanded on bail, bail is not an absolute right, but a privilege to be granted. Until the mid-1970s, there was no presumption in English law that a judge or magistrate should grant bail to those he remanded. It seemed to some reformers that this meant that the prison population was being unduly increased by 'unnecessary' remands in custody (the number of people remanded in custody before trial had increased by over 150 per cent in the previous decade). In 1976, therefore, the Government introduced a bill to change the balance of courts' decisions in favour of defendants getting bail and to require courts to give reasons for refusing bail. This bill became the Bail Act (in November 1976), which was first implemented in 1977.

Already, in 1975, the Home Office had sponsored projects, run by the New York based Vera Institute of Justice, based in Inner London and supported by the Inner London Probation Service, to test out ways of providing information to the courts (particularly magistrates' courts) about the community ties of defendants in the hope that this would assist magistrates and judges to grant bail to those they might otherwise have remanded in custody (primarily on a suspicion that they might otherwise have absconded). Community ties information had been developed in America by the Vera Institute to identify those defendants who could be predicted not to abscond on bail, and who could therefore be released in safety.[3]

The London projects were based on a magistrates' court and a remand prison, and the magistrates' court model was recommended by the Home Office to other courts. It was also studied by the Home Office Research Unit, which concluded that the scheme devised for giving courts information about community ties was a viable one, but was unable to demonstrate any reduction in the pilot court's use of custody arising from it.[4] It has been said, however, that the project's experiences were also useful to the framers of the 1976 Bail Act.

Although the Bail Act itself has now been in operation for over five years, it is difficult to tell whether either it or the provision of community ties information in magistrates' courts has had any effect on the numbers of defendants remanded in custody. The 1981 *Criminal Statistics* contain information about remands at the courts only since 1 January, 1978, and show a slight fall in magistrates' courts' proportionate use of custodial remands in respect of indictable offences over this period (from 17 per cent in 1979 to 15 per cent in 1981), even though the numbers actually remanded in custody grew from 38,000 to 42,000 during this period. The statistics for committal in custody for the preceding decade show that there was a drop in the rate at which custody was used; the main fall, however, occurred between 1975 and 1976 – before the Bail Act was passed – and so cannot be attributed to the Act itself, even if it *may* be related to the discussions which preceded the Act.[5] Indeed the proportion of committals for trial in custody has since grown from the 1977 low of 16 per cent to 19 per cent in 1979, 1980 and 1981.

In Inner London the provision of community ties information was undertaken by probation service staff and volunteers – although the organization of the scheme was criticized by the National Association of Probation Officers – and it has remained nationally one of the tasks of the probation service, although it may also be done or organized by other court staff. Such data as exist, however, suggest that the probation service's involvement in this process may be on the wane. The number of such 'Bail Information Reports' prepared by the probation service fell, according to the *Probation Statistics*, from about 3,000 in 1979 to 1,000 in 1981, although it rose in the following year to 1,700.[6]

At the same time, however, the probation service has been increasingly involved in the provision of accommodation for those on bail. In several probation areas bail hostels have been opened and many, probably most, probation hostels also take in bailees. These developments point to one possible effect of the 1976 Act and the provision of bail information. Both focused on the kind of decision made by judges and magistrates about remands in custody or bail and on the bases for these decisions. The process of providing bail information often involved, in the pilot project at least, probation staff in identifying community alternatives (particularly hostels) for otherwise homeless or rootless defendants at risk of a remand in custody, and it is probable that in some cases knowledge of the availability of such resources persuaded the police to *withdraw their objections to bail* before the case came to court.[7] Thus, while it is unlikely that the provision of bail information to courts is of much value against police objections to bail on the grounds that the defendant will offend, or interfere with prosecution witnesses, it may have helped to keep a group of homeless and rootless defendants from being remanded in custody. One might also hypothesize that the 1976 Act, by requiring the courts to give reasons for their decisions, has had a similar effect, and has also helped the courts not to accept uncritically (if they ever did) police objections to bail.

It seems likely, however, that these developments have had at best only a marginal effect in reducing or slowing the rate of increase in the numbers of defendants remanded in custody. A more promising line of development may be to reduce the need for remands at all by cutting out unnecessary delays in court proceedings. Recently, the Vera Institute of Justice has been working on such a project, designed to speed up the processing of cases through the magistrates' courts. This can be justified on economic grounds (providing speedier trials) and on moral grounds (justice should be seen to be done *quickly*, soon after the offence), but it may also have the merit of requiring fewer remands in custody.

One reason for hope is that early studies have suggested that many delays stem from the extreme slowness with which the police assemble and present the prosecution's case; there is evidence that they do not require the time they ask for through further remands. As remands where the police are assembling evidence are probably those where bail is most likely to be opposed by the police, it follows that a reduction in their number and frequency should lead to a cut in both the number of defendants remanded in custody and in the lengths of time they spend there.[8]

Even if it were possible to make a substantial reduction in the numbers remanded in custody before trial, our prisons would still contain many offenders who, it is generally agreed, should be dealt with by non-punitive community resources, rather than by custodial sentences out of proportion to their criminality. These include alcoholics, drug addicts and prisoners who are mentally ill, but the group that has attracted most of the recent attention is that described by the term 'persistent petty offenders'.

During the 1970s the Home Office identified persistent petty offenders, or 'socially inadequate offenders' (the two terms are not wholly synonymous), as a group who could usefully be diverted from prison without too much public protest. The basic idea was that many of the short prison sentences imposed by courts were for relatively trivial offences that merited custody only because of the persistence and frequency with which they were committed. Thus, these prison sentences were, in a way, a gesture of sentencers' exasperation with the offender, and with the system under which he or she was being sentenced, and did not exemplify the objectives of deterrence, retribution or rehabilitation. It was accepted that most of those so sentenced were people who were not 'criminals' but whose offending was a symptom or a by-product of their inability to cope with the 'formalities' of modern life. As such, it was often accompanied by other symptoms of the same condition, such as alcoholism and homelessness.[9] In effect, therefore, this argument has identified a class of individuals being processed by the courts which is not suitable for treatment within the prison system, but which may be amenable to it in the community.

In their origins, both day training centres and probation hostels (for adults) were aimed at this group. Day training centres were originally conceived as meeting 'the needs of the inadequate recidivist, whose behaviour and offences often reflect a lack of social development and tend to lead to a short succession of custodial sentences, apparently offering little benefit either to the offender or to the community'.[10] Similarly, the adult residents of probation hostels were defined, by an advisory committee in the Inner London Probation Service, as 'men with symptoms of inadequacy, immaturity, aggression and social irresponsibility, who lack appropriate family and community support'.[11] Both day training centres and probation hostels, however, have tended to concentrate on offenders who have more serious criminal records and are perhaps less 'inadequate' than the statements above suggest. Thus one potential strategy – special 'treatment' within the context of a probation order – failed to come to fruition.

In the late 1970s, therefore, the Home Office Research Unit studied various ways in which persistent petty offenders could be diverted from the criminal justice system in general, and prison in particular. It should be noted that the ideas underlying this study differed in certain crucial respects from those behind the original proposals for day training centres and probation hostels. The first difference was the abandonment of the ideal of 'treatment' in favour of a strategy of 'diversion'. The measures considered were not intended to 'cure' offenders of their inadequacy; they were not even necessarily intended to alleviate the symptoms; instead they were designed to steer these offenders away from the courts and away from prison. A second related difference was the change in emphasis from social inadequacy to persistent petty offending – the condition being now defined primarily by the offence rather than by the offender. Nevertheless, the research found that this group suffered multiple deprivations, being usually homeless, jobless and dependent on drink, as well as continually in trouble with the law.

The Home Office study concentrated on three possible diversion points:

the police – diverting from arrest and prosecution;

the courts – diverting from custodial sentences;

the prisons – diverting from further contact with the law.

The basis for this was an observation that a key factor in the cyclical process of offence–arrest–custodial sentence–offence is many petty offenders' lack of settled accommodation. Thus, if the cycle cannot be broken at the stages of arrest or sentencing, it was hoped that it might be by getting offenders accommodation on their release from prison.

The conclusions from the study of the practice of the police and magistrates' courts were that, in general, they tended to avoid arresting this group of persistent petty offenders and sending them to prison unless they were convinced they had no other options. Therefore only the introduction of other resources in the community would persuade police and magistrates to divert more offenders from the courts and prisons.

Specifically, the resources needed were shelters where drunks could be sent to sober up (most of the petty offences were connected with drinking – as an earlier Home Office study had shown),[12] and supportive services to contain persistent petty offenders in the community. The researcher, Suzan Fairhead, also commented that magistrates would need to have more confidence in the probation service's ability to work successfully with these offenders.[13]

The third element of the study was a project focused on persistent petty offenders when they had been discharged from prison. Its basic aim was to encourage them to refer themselves, or accept referral, to local accommodation facilities: after-care hostels, reception centres, landladies, hostels, etc. The project involved prison and probation staff together with volunteers who, in some cases, 'escorted' prisoners to accommodation.

The results of the project were disappointing. Only about a quarter of the persistent petty offenders involved were placed in accommodation, another quarter could not be found suitable places, and half rejected the help offered. Of those placed, only a quarter (8 out of 32) stayed in the chosen accommodation for longer than four weeks and a third did not even take up the offer made to them. Being placed in accommodation did not seem to lessen the risk of being reconvicted (perhaps because so few placements were at all successful), although some effect on sentencing was observed (in that those placed in accommodation tended to be treated more leniently). Thus, Suzan Fairhead commented, the results suggested a mismatch between clients' needs and the provision of resources. Her conclusion from this study was that persistent petty offenders could be diverted from custody more successfully by the provision of 'wet shelters' for them when they were drunk, and of day centres, run by the probation service, to contain and occupy them during the day.

This latter argument was developed in a further Home Office study, again by Suzan Fairhead, of probation day centres,[14] but it seems in part to be born out of desperation caused by the patent inadequacy of much of the accommodation available for homeless single people. Fairhead quotes the comment of one of the voluntary workers in the Home Office project: 'If this [reception centre] is all a man can be offered, there is not much incentive to keep out of prison.'[15] This aptly makes the point that a prison sentence is *not* necessarily the most degrading and inhuman experience that this group of persistent offenders may face.

The primary need, therefore, is for accommodation which can not only provide basic standards of care, but also give support and tolerance to help a difficult and deprived group. If this accommodation is available, then it is possible that day centres, whether run by the probation service or by other agencies, can help to provide somewhere to go, advice and opportunities to keep out of trouble, and perhaps even the chance to break out of a life-cycle of drinking and offending. Day-care in general rests on the assumption that those who go to the day centres have at least the fundamental right of stable or decent accommodation. Without that, however, there seems little chance for improvement, nor any reason to deny persistent petty offenders what little support even a prison can give.

This argument may seem a bizarre one, particularly in *this* book, but we must recognize that while it may be totally inappropriate to use the processes of law to deal with persistent petty offenders, the alternative at present may be worse. Suzan Fairhead, in her work, identified a particular confusion here between the helping and controlling elements of sentencing;[16] the lack of adequate provision helps to confound it. Our view also receives some support from

Stephen Shaw's 1980 analysis of the cost of penal sanctions.[17] One of the case examples he used to illustrate the varying costs of different sentences was of an unemployed single (separated) man sleeping rough or in 'common lodging houses'; Shaw compared the costs of a 28-day prison sentence with those of a hostel place and a probation order; his conclusion was that prison was not more expensive than a period of hostel residence. We would add that the hostel would probably be preferable on other grounds, as a more humane solution . . . except for the fact that there are relatively few hostels available by comparison with the number of prison places.

The accommodation problems of ex-prisoners extend, however, far beyond those who conform to the stereotype of the persistent petty offender. Research studies suggest that over a quarter of those discharged from prison have no stable accommodation to go to,[18] and some of these are men whose offending has been more serious, if persistent, than petty. For example, in one voluntarily-managed after-care hostel in South London, nearly half the residents (9 out of 21) had more than ten previous convictions and in the majority of cases their most recent conviction was for a serious offence (firearms, burglary, robbery, violence). Yet only two of them reoffended during their three-month stay at the hostel.[19] The point, therefore, is that accommodation has been and remains a key need for many ex-prisoners, a resource without which there is little hope of breaking the chain of offences.

Some offenders, particularly drug addicts and alcoholics, will need more specific resources than simply the provision of accommodation. As far as alcoholics are concerned, detoxification centres should be seen as merely part of the necessary provision. Many of those who are taken to them will be heavily dependent on alcohol and on the attendant way of life that has developed alongside it. Obviously it will be an improvement if someone is taken to a drying-out centre rather than to a police cell and then on to court, but the medical help which will be available there will not be compulsory and, whether it is accepted or not, there will be a need for an extensive range of back-up services. Facilities do exist now, but they are severely limited both by geographical location and by resources, often functioning on very low budgets and only with the help of dedicated short-term volunteers. More shelters are needed where food and temporary accommodation could be made available, particularly in the areas where alcoholics tend to gather, such as near railway stations and in shopping precincts. They could be manned by volunteers who would be able to provide help where needed, if only to advise clients on how to claim benefits, consult a doctor or contact their families. Alongside these hostels or shelters there is a pressing need for more long-term accommodation where similar help and access could be provided within an open, unpressurized, positive atmosphere in which respect for the person would be the guiding principle. At the present time the Simon and Cyrene communities run a series of such shelters, ranging from short-term provision through to long-term, more permanent communities, where participation is voluntary and the members may drop out if they wish and return when they need to.

Some of the hostels used for the accommodation of alcoholics are also used to provide shelter for drug addicts who share many of the personal and social problems experienced by those who depend on alcohol. Although there are drug clinics attached to hospitals throughout the country, they were set up to deal with registered addicts, the people known to have a dependency on heroin and other 'hard' drugs. They do make an important contribution, but are unable to touch many of the social problems experienced by addicts and they do not come into contact with large numbers of those who are addicted or experimenting. Support groups and the like are just as important for these people and, again, various projects do exist to provide shelter, advice and daytime accommodation.

One of the longest-running and most respected schemes is the Lifeline Project in Manchester. Lifeline opened in 1971 as a day centre 'to provide an immediate if short-term answer to the needs of a large group of chaotic and, for the most part, heavily intoxicated young drug users who were then to be found wandering aimlessly around the centre of Manchester'.[20] Although the agency's reputation in the drug treatment field grew rapidly, it stumbled from one financial crisis to another, with frequent cut-backs in staffing; its plans to open a residential rehabilitation facility were thwarted by local authority opposition and lack of funds. In 1975, when Lifeline was facing imminent closure, it approached NACRO and, after lengthy negotiations, it was agreed that the project should become a NACRO responsibility. When NACRO took over the management of Lifeline the next year, there was an opportunity for the project to re-evaluate its methodology and investigate the possibilities for providing a more comprehensive service for its clients. The most important new development to come out of this review, certainly in terms of providing an alternative to prison, was the Induction Programme. We shall discuss this in detail later; first, however, let us look at the philosophy that underlines all Lifeline's work.

'From its inception in 1971,' writes Rowdy Yates, the Project Co-ordinator,

> the Lifeline Project has maintained a clear, well-defined philosophy on the use of drugs. We have always maintained that addiction has

to do with the personality and attitude of the addict and little or nothing to do with any physical dependence which might develop to a particular substance. This means that recovery is dependent on fundamental change in the addict himself and that the individual can never be seen as the victim of addiction and must be encouraged to take responsibility for his attitudes and actions in order to understand the possibility of, and need for personal change. The Project therefore has a duty to refuse to allow its attenders to place themselves in powerless/victim/inadequate roles, to insist on the possibility of change, to refute the stereotype of a 'drug addict' which attenders themselves often cling to. Underlying this rigorous philosophy is the belief that people can 'get it right', that every drug user is capable of making momentous decisions about his/her life given the opportunity and the information necessary to reach that decision.

The Project has always maintained a strict no-drugs-on-the-premises rule, has never had a fixing room for addicts to inject themselves in and strictly discourages 'negative street-talk' about drugs. Furthermore, the Project has never accepted the arbitrary division between opiate users and 'the rest', has always seen its customers as poly-drug users and has insisted that the source of the drugs – be that Clinic, G.P., or the black market – is of secondary importance if indeed it has any relevance at all.

Much of the practical work of the Project revolves around the negotiating of formal and informal contracts relating to the behaviour, goals and needs of each attender. Agreement on aims and expectations defines the common ground wherein both the worker and the individual attenders can find room to manoeuvre and develop. Thus attenders are assisted in exploring realistic ways in which they might benefit from continued attendance. . . .

For many people who have used drugs consistently for a number of years, the idea of being in control of one's life becomes almost an alien concept, and he/she inevitably begins unconsciously to compensate through seeking more and more support from the drug sub-culture and the use of drugs. Drug use ceases to be mere entertainment and becomes an essential ingredient in the emotional make-up of the individual, providing feelings of security and self-worth.

The work of the Project must therefore be to assist attenders in becoming aware of their real feelings and so put them in touch with their own personal potential. Often this can best be done by challenging those statements and actions which appear to stem from the attender's 'street image' rather than the person that he/she really is. This is crucial, since to allow such behaviour to

> pass unchallenged would be to tacitly collude with, and thus strengthen attitudes which make it almost impossible for the individual to feel fulfilled without the support of drug use. Informal group structures also provide opportunities for developing critical appraisal actually within the sub-culture. In this way the Project can provide a confrontive environment and, because it is not a power situation (the Project has no control over the attender's supply of drugs, his/her chances of staying out of prison, etc.), more honest and straightforward relationships can be developed.[21]

The axis of Lifeline remains the day centre. It is the first point of contact for the drug user. Lifeline is the last drugs agency in Britain to retain a day centre facility, and it has done so because it believes that 'provision for those who are not even "motivated" enough to make and keep an appointment is crucial and only a drop-in facility can ensure this type of provision in a way which allows its users to choose for themselves whether they wish to use it'.[22]

> Day Centre services are available to attenders on three different levels. Firstly the reception area is reserved for those either too intoxicated to make constructive use of the other Day Centre facilities, or who are simply using the Project as a base, and can thus be expected to be entering and re-entering the premises on a number of occasions during any one day. This area is manned by all the Project staff on a rota basis and is kept deliberately spartan. Secondly, the Day Centre area itself offers a free midday meal, tea and coffee, table tennis, a pool table, library and laundry facilities, etc. The Day Centre workers have been careful to avoid 'free handouts' and the meal is thus seen as an exercise in learning to prepare cheap, nutritious food, whilst a nominal charge is made for laundry facilities. . . . Thirdly, the Project houses a small workshop which is used primarily by those attending the Induction Programme but is also available for use by Day Centre attenders.
>
> Transgression of the basic rules, by bringing drugs into the Project, violent behaviour, etc., is countered by automatic expulsion from the Project for a minimum of one day. Generally speaking, readmission will only be allowed on completion of a 'work contract'. A work contract will usually include both physical work and an exercise . . . designed to stimulate the imagination and provide a foundation for a discussion about future use of the Project.[23]

From the very beginning, Lifeline has seen a major part of its work as referring on to long-term rehabilitation those drug-users who profess a desire to stop using drugs. However, rehabilitation, of whatever kind, has been bedevilled by a high drop-out rate during its early stages. The drug-user will enter the rehabilitation programme with little or no formal preparation and having had no opportunity to discuss his or her motivation or indeed to select an appropriate facility from among the range available. (In Britain residential facilities can be divided roughly into concept-based therapeutic communities based loosely on the models of Phoenix House in New York and Daytop Village, and projects which operate what might be called a 'caring family' ethos.) It was to counter this problem that Lifeline instigated its Induction Programme in 1976.

> The Induction Programme is highly structured and lasts for two weeks. During this time the Inductee is expected to comply with three major conditions:
>
> To use no drugs or alcohol,
>
> To reside in a supervised hostel,
>
> To attend the Project daily.
>
> The hostel place is arranged by the Induction/Court work team who also liaise with, and support, the staff of each hostel. Whilst attending the Project Inductees are given a variety of work projects (including cleaning and maintenance, furniture renovation, etc.) and written work (life-stories, future plans, etc.), some of which are given as set tasks for evenings and weekends. In addition, each Inductee is given a counselling experiential therapy session (either individually or within the Induction group) every day.
>
> The majority of Inductions are undertaken on Bail and in these cases the three conditions are written into the Bail Order. At the end of the two weeks, each Inductee will have made a decision regarding their immediate future, and where this involves referral to a residential rehabilitation house, he/she will have some understanding of the concepts and structure of that house and how this will affect them.[24]

When the Induction Programme was first conceived, although most referrals came from the probation service, a fairly even balance was maintained between voluntary inductions and those completed on bail. Recently, however, as illicit drugs, particularly imported heroin, have become increasingly available, drug-users have been turning more and more to the black market and away from legitimate (or semi-legitimate) sources of supply. This has meant that the drug sub-culture has become more criminally orientated, a trend that has been reflected in referrals to Lifeline's Induction Programme. In 1980/81 four inductions were undertaken voluntarily and twenty-two as a requirement of bail; in 1981/82 the figures were six and nineteen respectively.

The staff of the Induction Department have a close working relationship with the probation service and with court liaison officers. They also maintain contact with local police forces and have had referrals from Lancashire, Merseyside and Greater Manchester drug squads. An increasing proportion of their caseload is made up of people who have been imprisoned, and they are heavily involved in 'through-sentence contact work'. They are increasingly being asked to support individual applications for parole, with induction as part of a parole package, or to provide post-sentence induction programmes for individuals on their release.

Lifeline's Induction Programme is the only venture of its type in the drug treatment field in Britain. It has been criticized by other professionals, chiefly on the grounds that it is not beneficial to defer the actual point of referral to a residential facility. What is not in doubt is that prison is not the place to treat drug abusers. Custodial sentencing rarely has any deterrent effects on an individual's desire to use drugs. Often, in fact, the effect is quite the opposite, since the drug subculture has come to regard sentences of imprisonment as an achievement of status and many commentators have noted that some drugs are as readily available in prison as in the community at large.

As Rowdy Yates remarks in *Out from the Shadows* (1981):

> . . . Imprisonment is a particularly inappropriate arena for the treatment of addiction. The Parliamentary All-Party Penal Affairs Group reported that: 'There is general agreement within the prison service that in itself prison is no treatment for drug dependence, and there are few serious attempts at therapy for drug dependents in custody. . . . All too often imprisonment does nothing to help the drug user deal with the problems of which drug-taking is a symptom, and on release the quickest way back to apparent friendship and status is through the drug scene.' Unfortunately, most drug users fail to take into account the lowering of their personal tolerance level during imprisonment and the search for 'apparent friendship and status' is often marked by overdose through acute poisoning. . . . However, despite all the available evidence and in the face of alarming re-addiction rates, prison continues to be the major resource for the 'treatment' of the majority of drug-users in this country.[25]

The latest (September 1983) report from Lifeline's Induction Department makes depressing reading. While noting a 'dramatic increase in the black market' and a 'consequent rise in referral to all parts of the Project', they also report that 'Recently published guidelines on sentencing formulated by Lord Chief Justice Lane have had an immediate impact in the courts. Many potential Inductees have already been imprisoned for periods between 3 and 7 years.'[26] And while drug users continue to be imprisoned, the organizations and agencies that *can* help them, be they residual rehabilitation houses or 'drop-in' centres and 'street aid' organizations, are fighting a losing battle to cope with increasing caseloads on ever-shrinking funds. Such facilities are more effective than imprisonment, both in terms of cost and in terms of the rehabilitative results achieved, yet it seems to be much easier to condemn a drug-taker or a persistent drunk to a prison cell or to deflect the debate by quoting the profits made by the professional 'pushers' than to seek out and support financially appropriate methods of coping with what is a socio-medical problem.

Similar points apply to the sentencing of 'mentally abnormal' offenders. The law recognizes that offenders who are officially described as mentally abnormal should receive special treatment. This treatment appears to run on a scale, dependent on the degree of mental illness assessed, and therefore the need for treatment, as follows:

'High need': Broadmoor or Rampton special hospitals;

'Medium need': probation order with condition of psychiatric treatment;

'Low need': 'voluntary' psychiatric treatment in the community or in prison.

It is noteworthy that this model has points in common with Pauline Hardiker's description of the position of probation in sentencing, in that the ability of a 'psychiatric probation order' to meet assessed treatment needs may be a more important factor in the sentencing decision than the degree to which the offence itself merited a custodial sentence.[27]

In fact, the courts' use of probation orders with conditions that the client should attend a course of in-patient or out-patient psychiatric treatment has been fairly constant over time – in 1982 approximately 1,200 orders with non-residential treatment requirements, and about 270 with residential treatment requirements, were made, compared with 1,200 and 280 the previous year, and about 1,000 and 340 in 1979. Overall, this represents between 4 and 5 per cent of all probation orders made. If there is any consistent trend in these figures, it is for the number of orders with residential treatment conditions to fall faster than the number of non-residential orders. Indeed, even the upturn in probation orders recorded in 1980 and 1981 did not bring about any growth in the use of conditions of in-patient psychiatric treatment.[28] This is probably not surprising, given that the trend in psychiatric services is generally away from institutionalized and towards community-based treatment, and given also the doubts that have been expressed about the general value of 'treatment'.

American research, however, has suggested that the rate of offending among those described as mentally ill may not be substantially different from that in the community at large.[29] If this is also the case in England, then we would expect to see the courts' use of psychiatric disposals rise in parallel with the growth in the number of offenders sentenced. That this has not happened is perhaps attributable most to changes in psychiatrists' views about who is 'treatable'. In general, courts make psychiatric disposals only on the recommendation of a psychiatric report, and it may well be that while the number of mentally ill offenders being processed by the criminal justice system is growing as fast as the total number of people coming before the courts, these reports are describing many of them as untreatable, or not mentally ill.

Some may regard this as a wholly admirable development, in that it avoids burdening people with the stigma of mental illness as well as that of offending, while others may see it as an entirely proper limitation on the use of treatment. Nevertheless, if mental illness is not solely a condition defined at psychiatrists' whims, but has some objective reality, then we should also be concerned that for mentally ill, as for persistent petty, offenders, there is a 'mismatch' between needs and the services available.

NOTES AND REFERENCES

1 Home Office, *Prison Statistics, England and Wales 1982*, London: HMSO, 1983.

2 Home Office, *Criminal Statistics, England and Wales 1980*, London: HMSO, 1981.

3 Vera Institute of Justice, *Programs in Criminal Justice Reform: Ten-Year Report 1961–71*, New York: Vera Institute of Justice, 1972.

4 See C. Simpson, 'Community Ties and the Bail Decision', *Justice of the Peace*, Vol. 141, Nos. 14 and 15, 1977, pp. 194–6 and 212–3.

5 Home Office, *Criminal Statistics, England and Wales 1981*, London: HMSO, 1982.

6 Home Office, *Probation Statistics, England and Wales 1982*, London: Home Office, 1984.

7 See Inner London Probation and After-Care Service, *ILPAS '76*, London: ILPAS, 1976.

8 See T.W. Church, 'The Costs of Adjournments in Magistrates' Courts', *Justice of the Peace*, Vol. 146, No. 30, 1982, pp. 445–50.

9 S. Fairhead, *Persistent Petty Offenders*, Home Office Research Study No. 66, London: HMSO, 1981.

10 Inner London Probation and After-Care Service, *ILPAS '76*, op. cit.

11 Ibid., p. 71.

12 J. Holborn, 'Casework with Short-Term Prisoners', in *Some Male Offenders' Problems*, Home Office Research Study No. 28, London: HMSO, 1975.

13 S. Fairhead, *Persistent Petty Offenders*, op. cit.

14 S. Fairhead, *Day Centres for Offenders*, Home Office Research Unit Paper No. 4, London: HMSO, 1981.

15 S. Fairhead, *Persistent Petty Offenders*, op. cit.

16 Ibid.

17 S. Shaw, *Paying the Penalty: The Cost of Penal Sanctions*, London: NACRO, 1980.

18 See R. Walmsley, *Steps from Prison*, London: ILPAS, 1972, and J. Corden, J. Kuipers and K. Wilson, *After Prison: A Study of the Post-Release Experiences of Discharged Prisoners*, University of York Department of Social Administration, Papers in Community Studies No. 21, 1978.

19 Inner London Probation and After-Care Service, *The Hill House Day Centre Project: A Review*, London: ILPAS, 1982.

20 R. Yates, *Out from the Shadows*, Lifeline Project 10th Anniversary Report, London: NACRO, 1981, p. 15.

21 Ibid., pp. 16–18.

22 Ibid., p. 19.

23 Ibid.

24 Ibid., p. 20.

25 Ibid., p. 12.

26 The Lifeline Project, Induction Department, *Interim Statistical Report*, September 1983.

27 P. Hardiker, 'Social Work Ideologies in the Probation Service', *British Journal of Social Work*, Vol. 7 No. 2, 1977, pp. 131–54.

28 Home Office, *Probation Statistics, England and Wales, 1982,* op. cit.

29 See M.J. Lillyquist, *Understanding and Changing Criminal Behavior*, New Jersey: Prentice-Hall, 1980, pp. 77–8.

Chapter Eight

FOREIGN EXAMPLES?

In this chapter we take a brief look at alternatives to custody in other countries and criminal jurisdictions. Broadly, these fall into two categories – legal and judicial systems that appear to rely less on prison than we do, and community-based projects to provide direct or indirect alternatives to custody. (It is something of a paradox that most of our examples of the latter come from the USA, a country that has one of the highest prison populations in the developed world, but, as we shall see later, there are reasons for this.)

We have relied in this brief comparative essay mostly on examples, analogies and parallels from Western Europe and North America. We would justify this by arguing that the general problems of crimes and punishments, and the informal systems of social control that underlie them, are more similar in these countries than they are in the states of Eastern Europe or Japan, the developing or underdeveloped countries. Consideration of examples 'closer to home' should therefore be less likely to lead us into false assumptions about what it may be possible to achieve here.

We must observe, however, that the criminal justice systems of apparently alien societies can exhibit forms that seem very close to English theory and practice. Consider the following description of a work-study school for juvenile delinquents in China:

> The school is serious in expecting the students to make three breakthroughs: to observe discipline and live as members of a collective; to break away from former gang buddies; to try to understand why they went wrong; to search for causes both within themselves and in their environment.[1]

In their emphasis on criminal influences and internal causes of delinquency, as well as on the virtues of discipline and group living, Chinese work-study schools (to which offenders are sent for indeterminate periods, until they have reformed) seem to have many points of similarity with some of our own custodial or quasi-custodial institutions for juveniles. The greatest differences between the Chinese and English systems for dealing with juvenile offenders appear to lie in the processes that take place between offence and incarceration. In China, much petty crime by juveniles seems to be dealt with through forms of counselling and mediation without police involvement; even if the police are involved they may decide not to prosecute, according to the attitude of the offender. Sentencing, however, appears to be entirely institutional – offenders are sent to work-study schools or reformatories, depending on the seriousness of the offence. Thus, much of the intervention that in England is used instead of a custodial sentence, in China appears to take place before any kind of criminal process has begun and may divert offenders from it. Yet the Chinese system of juvenile justice nevertheless appears to require institutions to 'reform' those offenders who are not diverted from it.

This brief resumé serves to make several general points about non-custodial alternatives in other jurisdictions. Firstly, the elements of diversion, intervention (by social workers or their approximate equivalents) and the final recourse to some form of custody, appear to be common to all of them, even if they may appear at differing stages in the process – before, after or instead of a formal court hearing. Secondly, it may be difficult to replicate programmes 'imported' from other systems in England, where some of the fundamental assumptions on which they are based may not be true in practice. Thirdly, while other countries may have developed better strategies than we have for dealing with offenders, most of them are implemented in the context of courts having the power to incarcerate offenders.

The penal system in England and Wales is justly criticized for keeping so many people in prison by comparison with other European countries. A recent analysis of the prison statistics of eight European countries by Ken Pease and Catherine Fitzmaurice suggests that the number of adult prisoners under sentence is higher, relative to the countries' populations, in England than in Scotland, Switzerland, Belgium, France or the Netherlands. (Only Northern Ireland and Sweden had more adults in prison.) This is attributable primarily to the fact that courts in England and Wales pass *longer* prison sentences than do the courts of all the eight countries except Northern Ireland and France. Pease and Fitzmaurice argue from this that if English and Welsh courts were to adopt the sentencing policies of Sweden, Belgium, Scotland, Switzerland or the Netherlands, but still send the same percentage of offenders to prison, they would cut our adult sentenced prison population by half or more.[2]

This proposition leads on to the question of why, in societies that are more similar than different, the lengths of prison sentences should vary so much and, apparently, arbitrarily. Unfortunately there are no easy, complete answers to this question, but there are some factors that help explain these differences for some countries, and these in turn may give some guidance to the adoption or rejection by us of their sentencing policies.

The first and most obvious point is that those countries that have lower adult prison populations and/or policies of shorter sentences have legal systems based on a different model from the adversarial one of English and American law. Continental law is based on an 'inquisitional' system, where questions of guilt and innocence are established not through the forensic skills of the advocates for the prosecution and defence, but through questioning by a judge or magistrate (who in the English system is, in theory, more like a referee in a trial by combat). In practice, the two kinds of systems are probably much *less* dissimilar than this bald epitome suggests, and the experience of being tried in a French *tribunal correctionel* may not be unlike its counterpart in a London magistrates' court.[3]

It has been argued. however, that in the inquisitional system there is less pressure on defendants to enter a plea of guilty to a lesser offence, in the hope of obtaining a more lenient sentence. We suggest that, if this were the case, then justice would be seen to be done more often, and courts would be less tempted to impose exemplary sentences on those who *were* convicted of the crimes of which they were accused. In reality, however, continental courts appear to have developed their own ways of giving speedy trials to 'co-operative' defendants. In France, for example, there are two grades of offence: the more serious *crimes*, tried in the *cour d'assises* and the less serious *délits* tried in the *tribunal correctionel. Crimes* carry a mandatory minimum five-year custodial sentence (which may be reduced for extenuating circumstances); perhaps because of this, many serious offences are dealt with as if they were *délits* before the *tribunal correctionel*, which has more limiting sentencing powers. This pretence that some offences are less serious than they really are may be regarded partly as a device to deal with cases more expeditiously, partly to leave the *cour d'assises* to deal with complex or very serious offences, and partly perhaps to avoid the mandatory custodial sentences of the latter (although in practice, because of mitigation, the actual differences in sentence lengths are less than one would expect).[4]

French courts are perhaps not a good example, because in fact they tend to pass relatively few custodial sentences (although those that they do pass tend to be long in duration). The practice described above (which appears to be technically illegal) does illustrate, however, that the inquisitional system may also have its defects. The mandatory (in theory) five-year minimum sentence for *crimes* also serves to introduce a doctrine that may be more important in setting sentence lengths than the form of law under which an offender is tried. This is the doctrine that we here call 'legalism'.

Essentially, 'legalism' in this context means the supremacy of legislation over judicial discretion in fixing the lengths of sentences. Associated with this are the principles that all sentences should conform to a fixed tariff, and that custodial sentences should be determinate in length, Legalism appears to rest not on popular, or presumed popular, sentiments about the role of punishment in sentencing, but on liberal views about the rule of law. Associated with legalism appears to be a belief that punishment in sentencing should be the minimum necessary to show society's disapproval of the offence. By contrast with our system, treatment, deterrence, revenge and incapacitation are much less strongly emphasized as sentencing objectives. Inkeri Antilla has described the principles of punishment in the Finnish criminal code as follows:

Punishment

'should not be cruel';

'should reflect the principles of proportionality and equality';

'should be directed at the offender alone';

'should not cause needless suffering';

'should not cause unregulated cumulation of sanctions';

'should be economical from the point of view of society'.[5]

Similarly, the criteria used in the Netherlands for deciding whether to adopt a new non-custodial sentence take into account such factors as whether the new alternative will reduce the courts' use of custody, whether it fits into the 'tariff' and whether it increases public control over the penal system. The treatment, deterrent, incapacitating or controlling elements of the sentence – items that would be emphasized in England and Wales – appear to be relatively insignificant in the process of Dutch criminal reform by comparison with ideas related to fairness and equality.[6]

We suggest that, in northern European countries at least, the doctrine of legalism has aided the development of relatively short prison sentences for adults.

Unfortunately, the importation of such a doctrine into English penal policy would probably not cut the courts' use of prison sentences. We have already mentioned, in our discussion of parole, the disastrous consequences in America of state legislatures limiting courts' discretion in sentencing. As chronicled by Roger Hood, the net effect has been to increase the length of prison sentences and therefore raise the prison population.[7] Merely to assert that in England and Wales Parliament should control sentences more strictly by law could be counter-productive. Indeed, the provisions for youth custody in the 1982 Criminal Justice Act stem in part from the anomalies created by statutory limitations on the courts' ability to sentence young offenders.[8]

It also appears to be the case that courts in countries where prison sentences are short are *more* likely to use custody as a sanction. Thus, from the comparative figures presented by Pease and Fitzmaurice, it appears that the four countries with the shortest average effective sentence lengths (between about seven weeks and five months) – Sweden, Scotland, Switzerland and the Netherlands – also recorded more receptions into prison under sentence (between 100 and 129 receptions per 100,000 population) than did the four countries – Belgium, England and Wales, France and Northern Ireland – where average prison sentences were longer (between five and a half months and seventeen months).[9] This association between short prison sentences and high use of custody suggests that policies to shorten sentence lengths could result in the courts sending more offenders to prison, if for shorter sentences. Indeed, the new provisions for youth custody and detention sentences in the 1982 Criminal Justice Act appear to contain just such an invitation to courts to put young offenders away for brief periods 'to teach them a lesson' (in the expectation that any damage done can be repaired by supervision from a probation officer or social worker).

One reason for the high rates of prison sentencing in some European countries may be that these sentences are used for offences that are treated very differently in England and Wales. In Sweden, for example, in 1978, the 10,500 'institutional' sentences (over two-thirds of which were for periods of under four months) were distributed over offence types as follows (the approximate English and Welsh equivalents for 1980 are given in parentheses):

	Sweden (1978)	*(England & Wales (1980))*
Prison sentences for:		
Drunken driving	34%	(6%)*
Larceny	20%	(41%)
Violence	14%	(11%)
Fraud	4%	(7%)
Drug offences	4%	N/A
Others	24%	(35%)

* All motoring offences

While some of the apparent differences shown between Swedish and English/Welsh sentencing are due to the difficulty of identifying exactly corresponding types of offences, it is clear that Swedish courts are very much more ready than English ones (given that the former appear to impose prison sentences roughly twice as often) to use custody as a sanction for drunken driving, but less ready to use it for property offences.

By contrast, the distribution of offences among probation orders was as follows:

	Sweden (1978)	*(England & Wales (1980))*
Probation orders for:		
Drunken driving	9%	(2%)*
Larceny	49%	(64%)
Violence	9%	(9%)
Fraud	17%	(7%)
Drug offences	3%	N/A
Others	13%	(18%)

* All motoring offences

and the ratio of prison sentences to probation orders is:[10]

	Sweden (1978)	*(England/Wales (1980))*
Number of prison sentences per probation order for:		
Drunken driving	6.53	(3.38)*
Larceny	0.67	(1.31)
Violence	2.52	(2.24)
Fraud	0.40	(1.29)
Other offences	2.87	(1.10)
All offences	1.65	(1.40)

* All motoring offences.

These figures show that, while the relative use of prison sentences and probation orders is about the same in Sweden as in England, with both countries using the former more often than the latter, there are considerable differences between types of offences. Swedish courts are more likely to use probation than prison for property offences than are English courts, but use prison six times as often as probation as a sanction against drunken driving. These statistics reflect the very different emphases in Sweden and England on the relative merits of prison and probation for property offenders, and suggest that there is no absolute reason why thefts, burglaries and even robberies should attract the sanction of imprisonment so often in England and Wales.

Inevitably, however, we are forced to conclude that while European and other legal systems may show us valuable models that contrast with English sentencing practice, they are less helpful than has been suggested in pointing towards definite policies and projects to reduce courts' use of custody.[11] For those, it seems, we should perhaps turn to America. We have already commented on the seeming paradox of a country with a very high prison population giving us examples of ways to reduce the use of custody. In fact there are several reasons why we should take American examples seriously, even if we do not believe that they can be imported wholesale and unchanged into the English system.

The first reason is that the problem of overcrowding in American prisons is at least as serious as in England and Wales (even if the institutions themselves are not always as old and dilapidated), and so attempts to resolve the problem are likely to be just as urgent and serious.

The second reason is that American courts have *fewer* sentencing options open to them for the more serious offences: essentially they can imprison an offender or place him or her on probation.[12] Probation caseloads are generally high, and decisions to make a probation order are not necessarily related to the offender's perceived need for social work help or treatment. The job of the probation officer is therefore more overtly one of surveillance and social control. In this, probation officers often delegate the provision of social work help, where needed, to other, community-based agencies (or to specialist workers within their own agency). As the majority of their clients are poor, disadvantaged and from ethnic minorities, this can lead to the development of a variety of community projects aimed at diverting offenders from custody.

This pluralism of intervention may also stem from differences between the criminal justice systems in different states; a decisive reform such as the virtual abolition of custodial institutions for juveniles in Massachusetts may be easier to achieve in such a situation than in the less diverse English jurisdiction.

In addition, the US Government embarked on a programme of sponsoring the development and testing of community initiatives to improve all aspects of the operation of the criminal justice system. While this work appears to have had little significant impact on the system itself, the rigour with which some projects (but not all) have been evaluated has added significantly to our knowledge of how alternative strategies succeed or fail.

Finally, the strong tradition of 'self-help' that has developed in America – and indeed has been mandated by the need to supplement state-funded 'welfare' agencies[13] – has provided a climate within which such initiatives can flourish. This is important, because the recent history of the reforms of sentencing attempted in England and Wales has suggested that such 'dirigiste' policies fail (in part at least) to achieve their objectives and often have undesirable, and apparently unforeseen, consequences.

The American initiatives that are presented here are necessarily only examples that may help us to learn some lessons to our own benefit. They focus not only on providing alternatives to custodial sentencing, but also on diverting putative offenders from criminal proceedings of any kind.

The most dramatic of these initiatives was the effective closure of all but a few custodial and residential institutions for juveniles in Massachusetts. Faced with overcrowded institutions, reports of extreme brutalities committed by the staff, and a recidivism rate of 80 per cent, the Director of the Department of Youth Services, Dr Jerome Miller, set in motion this unprecedented change between 1970 and 1972. (The last Massachusetts training school closed in 1975.) He had been appointed in 1969 to reform the institutions, but his attempts to introduce a more liberal and humane approach met resistance from staff employed in the schools, who accused him of undermining discipline. Liberalization seemed doomed to failure, so Miller emptied the institutions by paroling and transferring their inmates to alternative programmes and giving leave of absence to their superintendents. A small number of children are still held in secure institutions, but, for the majority, a wide range of community facilities has been developed.

This 'experiment' was evaluated by Harvard University; essentially the evaluation found that the virtual abolition of custody and of residential treatment for juveniles had had no impact on crime rates or on the reconviction rates of youths processed by the juvenile justice system.[14] This, in turn, suggests that the Massachusetts initiative could be implemented in other jurisdictions. It would be true to say, however, that the reform owed a great deal to the intervention and action of Dr Miller and some of his staff, in response to known failings and abuses of the institutional system, and less to theoretical critiques of the preceding regime of treatment, and relatively little to initiatives from within that existing system. For this reason, while the experiment seems eminently replicable, we doubt that it will be repeated often; more gradual reforms, with all their failings, seem more likely to be common. Nevertheless, it is worth noting that some English social services departments are adopting policies that are in some ways analogous to those of Massachusetts in their aims, although not in the way they have been introduced, and are attempting to move the care of children from institutions into the community.[15] Thus, if there is the will to close institutions, ways may be found to provide equally effective support in the community.

A different kind of project can be seen in the Chicago Unified Delinquency Intervention Services project. UDIS was set up in October 1974 as an experiment to provide an alternative to incarceration. The typical subject was a young person living in inner-city Chicago, Illinois, who had repeatedly been in trouble with the police and who would have been sent to one of the seven state youth correctional establishments. In Cook County, where the programme was based, it was argued that there was a need to co-ordinate those resources aimed at helping young people; prior to UDIS the various facilities had been diffused between private and public agencies including, among others, street-aid-type organizations, church groups and school-based programmes.

In the report on the project produced for the funding body (Illinois Law Enforcement Commission),[16] the principles upon which the project was based are set out as follows:

> 'The least drastic alternative principle' was to be the centrepiece of the UDIS approach; given a choice, UDIS would put the youth in the environment least unlike his normal one. Keeping the youth at home was less drastic than taking him away from home; providing services in the community was less drastic than providing him with services located elsewhere; and letting the youth retain freedom of movement was less drastic than instituting compulsory controls.
>
> Next, the UDIS approach was to get the youth out of the juvenile justice system fast – within six months if possible. Long-term care was not to the UDIS's style. The urgings of service providers that 'just a few more weeks' in a programme would produce the desired effects were to be resisted.
>
> The third key principle of the UDIS approach was to be individualized programming. Detailed work-ups on each case were to be conducted, going beyond the social and family investigations that the courts or the welfare agencies had conducted. They were also to come at the situation from a fresh perspective: to ascertain the strengths in the youth and the reinforcing elements in his environment, not to catalogue deficiencies. Once this was done. the UDIS participant could get the programming he or she required. Progress would be monitored closely by a Case Manager with a relatively small caseload, and it would be possible to make changes quickly when indicated.

UDIS's ultimate objectives were to reduce delinquency among its youth, with all that implies about other positive changes in the youth's outlook and behaviour, and to reduce commitments to the Juvenile Division of the Department of Corrections (usually called simply 'DOC') by 35%.

In 1973 Dr Jerome Miller, from Massachusetts, was appointed as the Director of the Department of Children and Family Service and, although he held this post for only a short period, his first major move was to bring back into Illinois a large number of children who had been placed in institutions outside the state boundaries. But UDIS never planned to undertake anything as drastic as the closing of institutions that had been carried out in Massachusetts; instead it aimed at the 35 per cent who could otherwise have been committed from the state's largest county. It was intended to deal not so much with the less serious offender as with those cases where there were doubts about making a committal. Those involved in initiating the project acknowledged the fact that there had been previous efforts to reduce crime which had focused on the 'chronic delinquent':

> But a variety of research barriers have typically obstructed efforts to learn from them. Sometimes the programmes have been scattered, sometimes too limited in scope. Or often the test environment has been too soft . . . the programmes have dealt with suburbia, not the inner city; the status offender, not the truly inveterate delinquent; or has been an alternative to probation, not incarceration. UDIS, with its Chicago setting, a coherent and innovative approach, its varied services, and a mandate to deal with the committable delinquent, provided a unique prototype to examine.

The following extracts from the report will give some idea of what the programme was about.

> The menu of vendor services available to UDIS Case Managers fell into six categories: advocacy, counselling, educational/vocational, group homes/foster care, rural programmes, and intensive care . . .

> *Advocacy* . . . is a relatively recent concept in juvenile services. It refers to the role of representing the youth in his confrontation with the juvenile justice system or any other of the institutions he may encounter. An analogy is often drawn between this role and that of the typical middle-class parent whose child is picked up by

the police. The parent may be angry or may be supportive, but he or she will go to the police station, make the necessary commitments to the authorities, get a lawyer if the offence is a serious one, arrange for treatment services if indicated, and generally run the interference that keeps most middle-class delinquents out of training schools. Advocacy services were intended to provide the UDIS youth with a person who could fill a similar role in dealing with the system. . . . The UDIS and advocacy philosophies were compatible: both acknowledged the role of their clients as victims as well as offenders – victims of neglect, poor schools, peer pressures, and institutions of social control . . . but there was also a highly pragmatic reason for the importance of advocacy in the UDIS service roster. UDIS had to demonstrate first that it could offer more intensive personal contact than a probation officer could and, second, that it could provide surveillance while the youth was in the community to protect public safety. . . .

Counselling Services were intended to help the youth reconcile the conflicts in his life. Unlike the street-oriented advocacy services that focused on informal contact between the para-professional worker and the youth, the counselling services offered scheduled weekly or twice-weekly sessions with professional counsellors. . . .

Educational/Vocational Training. With only a handful of exceptions UDIS referrals had school problems. Truancy and poor school performance were nearly universal among the members of the sample, and a number of personal history folders also made reference to learning handicaps or mental deficiencies. UDIS therefore from the beginning maintained contacts with academic services. In broad terms, these services fell under two headings: tutorial programmes, which worked with students on a one-to-one basis, and alternative schools, which provided a normal class structure with special supplementary resources for problem youth. Both types of services were designed to provide maximum learning in a minimum time – they had the UDIS youngsters for only a few months and were asked to compensate for years of academic deficiencies. . . . Vocational programmes (which included courses in welding, car mechanics, machine and raw material processing, and printing) were intended to prepare the older UDIS client for independent living by providing training and exposure to the world of work. The emphasis was on development of employable skills so that the UDIS youth who had egressed could realistically believe that the option of getting and holding a legitimate job was open to him.

In addition to these provisions (termed level I interventions) UDIS also ran group homes and foster care placements (termed level II interventions). The former were typically large old houses with about eight young people in residence, usually with houseparents. A referral was likely to be made if an official (for example, a judge or probation officer) insisted on the child being removed from home as a condition of participating in the project. Other children were put into care of foster parents who had been recruited and screened and then trained to provide a counselling service for their charges. Level III interventions took the form of rural programmes and intensive residential care facilities. The rural programmes set out to give the youths an experience of a non-urban environment and provided outward-bound type exercises, vocational experiences and one exercise which allowed the participants to explore and compare rural and city environments. The other residential provision was designed to deal with those deemed to be in need of psychiatric or psychological evaluation and treatment and sometimes a judge would stipulate that a youth with a long offence record be placed in an intensive care programme if he was to be referred to UDIS.

It is not possible here to describe in full the research programme which was set up to test the operational 'success' of UDIS, but the main conclusions must, at least, be reported. The researchers concluded that:

> UDIS had a substantial effect in reducing DOC commitments from Cook County, very possibly meeting the . . . 35% objective.
>
> If the question is whether UDIS implemented the three principles that were the underpinnings of this approach, the simplest answers seem to be these. On individualized programming, UDIS Case Managers rated good marks for translating this objective into actual practice. . . . UDIS seldom opted for a residential or non-community service without a compelling reason; often UDIS was not given a choice . . . On short-term programming, UDIS retreated significantly from its original goal. Some of the reasons were similar to those that have motivated youth workers elsewhere, variations on the theme that a few more months, another try, might finally get the job done.[17]

It must be remembered that the most important concern was to reduce the level of delinquency and it was evaluated in these terms. The criterion of recidivism which was given most attention was not whether the subjects came in contact with the criminal justice system as a result of reoffending, but whether they were subsequently sentenced to incarceration. On this basis, when a UDIS sample was compared with a sample of young people sentenced to the Department of Corrections, the latter group seemed to have a slightly lower incidence of repeated offences, while the UDIS group demonstrated a slightly lower level of seriousness when offending reoccurred, claiming a marked superiority for the level III (residential) placement. The report contained a vast amount of detail on this sample and, while it recommended the continuation of the programme, it did see it as one part of a sequence of sentences that ought to be available, ranging from 'station adjustments' (police cautioning or other methods of initial diversion) for first offences, then probation, then UDIS, then committal. UDIS was concerned with those youths perceived to be at the more serious end of the spectrum, and many of the participants had a record of thirteen or more offences before being referred to UDIS. The results claimed that the post-intervention recidivism rate was substantially below that of pre-intervention offending.

A fall-off in the rate of seriousness of offending does not, in fact, seem to be an uncommon outcome of projects that have attempted to measure criminal behaviour before and after intervention.[18] It may demonstrate the ability of such projects to 'hold' their subjects away from offending for a while, or it may simply be an aspect of the fact that for many offenders their chances of being reconvicted tend in any case to decrease as they get older.

Several points can be made about the value and disadvantages of the UDIS approach. The project did seem to achieve a measure of increase in the use of community-based placements for young offenders; and within them a range of intervention strategies, in addition to counselling, were used. On the other hand, the results, in terms of recidivism, were less than conclusive, and the project could perhaps, in theory, have relied less on institutional placements than it did.

It is significant that 'on short-term programming UDIS retreated significantly from its original goal'.[19] If there is one thing that has emerged from post-war research into the effects of social work it is that more intervention does not necessarily mean better.[20] Thus it may be that the belief that 'another try might finally get the job done'[21] contributed to the inconclusive nature of the project's outcome.

A somewhat different approach, but still based on the proposition that the system could be redesigned to reduce the courts' use of custody, was adopted in California in the mid-1960s. The California Probation Subsidy Program was designed to give counties within the state a vested interest in reducing the number of committals to their local prisons and increasing the use of probation and other non-custodial programmes. Counties which reduced the number of committals to state establishments received a subsidy of approximately $4,000 for each person so diverted. These subsidies were to be used to create facilities for intensive supervision. At first this scheme focused on reducing probation caseloads in order to allow probation officers to spend more time on each client, but, as it developed, more use was made of programmes sited in local institutions and gradually these specialist caseloads were not limited to those who would have ended up in prison. At the same time, the feeling developed that intensive 'traditional' supervision of probationers on small caseloads could be counter-productive; this led to several different approaches to working with offenders being adopted, some more successfully than others. There was also a noticeable increase in the level of *county-based* incarceration as offenders were directed away from state prisons.

An evaluation of the subsidy programme was undertaken by staff of the Center of Administration of Criminal Justice at the University of California.[22] The study found that intensive probation supervision was at least as effective as state incarceration as indicated by recidivism rates for both juvenile and adult offenders and that there was no significant difference in the level of rehabilitative effectiveness between the new probation practices adopted under the subsidy and the traditional methods. In summary remarks it was stated that:

> Only a handful of the many possible approaches have been systematically tried and evaluated. If the choice now is to give up the attempt to develop programmes that will be effective in reducing recidivism or to continue to try to develop such programmes, it seems clear that the choice should be to continue to try.

At the same time, the California Youth Authority had been running the Community Treatment Program for young offenders. The object of this programme was to keep youngsters out of state institutions by placing them in a variety of non-custodial settings and projects. Placements were chosen according to a system of classifying young offenders with the aim of 'matching' the offender to the placement in order to maximize the effectiveness of the latter in reducing recidivism. The placements were oriented towards 'treatment' rather than towards other modes of social work intervention such as advocacy, and, perhaps consequently, there was a tendency to resort to institutions for those who did not 'respond' to their community placement.[23] Thus, in both the California projects, while the *immediate* aim of diversion from custody was achieved, some offenders were subsequently diverted *back* into other institutions. This tendency demonstrates the difficulty of sustaining such projects by remaking only a part of the system. It appears that, so long as there are institutions in which to place offenders, they will be used, in the name of care or of control.

A disillusionment with the 'treatment model' and other alternatives to imprisonment, combined with a desire to help the victims of crime, had led to a further examination, in the USA and elsewhere, of the ancient concept of restitution, whereby wrongdoers are required to make a payment of money or services to their victims. During 1976–7 the Law Enforcement Assistance Administration in the United States funded a number of pilot adult and juvenile restitution programmes to test whether it would be viable to introduce the concept more widely. One of the practical difficulties is to accurately assess the amount of restitution and these pilot programmes have had to determine methods for arriving at a sum acceptable to victim and offender alike. Where such schemes have been in operation one of two models was usually adopted:

1. *Arbitration* – a neutral arbitrator hears the details of the case from both the victim and the offender and arrives at a figure which is then binding on the offender but not necessarily on the victim, who may enter into a civil suit. Restitution schemes tend to concentrate only on out-of-pocket losses rather than dealing with compensatory sums for any pain or other distress, and this is why the option is left open to engage in a civil case.

2. *Negotiation* – the victim and the offender are brought together with a staff member employed by the project to negotiate a sum.

One problem with such schemes is that poorer offenders may find it inequitably more difficult and burdensome to make financial restitution to their victims; difficulties have also been perceived with enforcement. This in turn has meant that most American jurisdictions have made restitution a condition of a probation order, and in at least one area (Minnesota) restitutees have been kept in a correction centre – which may appear to defeat the object of the exercise.

On the other hand, a restitution scheme has an apparent benefit to the victim of a crime by giving him or her *more* control over the way the offence is treated than does the more impersonal and regular process of the criminal law alone. As such it seems to fit into (and was derived from) some elements of what we have characterized as the doctrine of 'legalism' in Europe. One criterion for evaluating a new sentence in the Netherlands, for example, is whether it enhances victims' participation and influence in the criminal justice system,[24] and it has been suggested[25] that one reason for the use of 'summary' proceedings in French courts for serious offences is that it gives better and speedier redress to the victim.

The Columbus Night Prosecutor's Program moved away from the concept of restitution following a court hearing, and a finding of guilt, by allowing both parties involved in a dispute to confront each other and arrive at a resolution *before* the offender was arrested. The method adopted when the scheme was set up was that if an offence of a certain type resulted from a dispute between two or more people, the 'night prosecutor' had discretion to divert the case to an administrative hearing before the City Prosecutor, who evaluated the statements of the parties and attempted to reach a resolution of the dispute.

The Columbus scheme was initiated in 1971. Five law lecturers were used as night prosecutors and law students acted first as observers and later as participants. When a person came to the police station to file a complaint he would be diverted into the Night Prosecutor's Program, where the complaint would be taken and a date given for the hearing. During the pilot stage (November 1971 – September 1972) one thousand hearings were scheduled and all but twenty cases were resolved without the need to file criminal charges. A grant of $80,000 was made available to fund the programme and it was expanded to include Saturday morning as well as the five evenings, and law students were used as hearing officers.

The hearing officer, complainant, respondent, lawyers (rarely needed) and witnesses were present at the hearing, which was informal. Each party had the right to tell his side of the story and the hearing officer acted as mediator. The parties were encouraged to suggest a solution, but, if they were unable to do so, the officer suggested a possible resolution. John Palmer (one of the founders of the programme and a member of the Law School of Capital University, Columbus) explained what happened if either or both of the parties failed to turn up for the hearing. If the person who had made the complaint failed to attend, the hearing officer interviewed the respondent and decided whether any further action was needed. If the position was reversed, the accuracy of basic facts (e.g. addresses, names) was checked and if a mistake had been made a new date was set for the hearing. In other cases the person who had filed the complaint would be encouraged to seek an alternative remedy.

In an article on the programme in *Federal Probation*,[26] Palmer provided examples of typical cases which had been dealt with at the hearings; one of these examples is reproduced here to give some idea of how the scheme operated.

> A familiar situation which results in a hearing involves an assault and battery by a husband on his wife. Frequently the woman will arrive in the Night Prosecutor's office soon after the battle has ended, complete with black eye and torn clothing. She usually wants to have her husband arrested right away and put into jail. Unless there is a very real danger that the husband is going to attack her or others again in the immediate future, the clerk usually explains the futility of an arrest. (In Columbus the bail for assault and battery is normally low enough so that anyone arrested on that charge will very likely be out on the street again in less than an hour after he is arrested. Through experience the staff have learned that, rather than providing a solution to the wife's problem, the fact that he has been arrested frequently infuriates the husband so much that he goes right back home and beats his wife again. Experience has also shown that it is generally the wife who later comes in and posts the bail money!) The clerk explains the hearing procedure, suggesting to the wife that the Night Prosecutor's Program offers the husband and wife a chance to discuss their problems in a calm, controlled setting with an unbiased party to mediate. The clerk points out that the hearing process may be a much more positive step which offers the possibility of long-term gains as opposed to the questionable value of having the husband thrown in jail.
>
> When the husband and wife appear for the hearing, the hearing officer allows them to express their hostilities, then talks with them about possible solutions. Usually the hearing officer will ask the couple if they want to continue the marriage or get a divorce. Most often neither party wants a divorce. The wife does not want her husband arrested; she simply wants him to stop beating her. The hearing officer points out to the husband the problems which he will encounter if he is arrested on an assault and battery charge, including the possibility of losing his job, obtaining a criminal arrest record, and suffering all the social stigmas that accompany such a record. If there are children, the hearing officer points out that the couple have the responsibility to give them as good an environment as possible in which to live. He may refer the couple to a counselling service or to other community agencies established to help citizens with whatever personal problems they are encountering.
>
> Frequently in such a hearing one partner will reveal problems in the marriage or feelings of which the other partner was not aware.

> The couples leave the Night Prosecutor's office in various frames of mind. Some of them are still hostile and threatening, but agree not to file charges at that time. Others admit to each other their shortcomings and leave with an agreement to try to work things out. Whatever their attitude, however, they have been given an opportunity which seldom is presented when the parties go directly to court.

In most of the cases described by Palmer, it seems unlikely that the wrongdoer would have received a custodial sentence, but there is no reason why this and similar schemes should not be used where there is a greater probability of incarceration resulting from a court appearance. Not only could it be used to avoid a prison sentence, but it can also divert an offender from gaining a criminal record and offers a route towards a solution satisfactory to both parties in a dispute.

The practice of diverting from court and thus from imprisonment can be applied to other types of offenders and offences as well. A summary report produced under the auspices of the US Department of Justice[27] suggests, in addition to 'Citizen Dispute Settlement' (of which the Night Prosecutor's Program is an example), programmes to divert 'public inebriates' to detoxification centres (as has been suggested for England), to 'retrain' drunken drivers and to provide extra assistance to combat 'vocational disadvantage' among young offenders.

Diversionary programmes have not been an unqualified success, however, and few projects have achieved all their objectives. The New York City Court Employment Project, run by the Vera Institute of New York, was based on providing education, training, counselling and job placements for disadvantaged young offenders. Those who went through the programme appeared to be less likely to reoffend, and more likely to be helped to find jobs. These jobs, however, were no better than those they had held already, and thus whatever its success in affecting the way its clients were processed by the criminal justice system, this project appeared unable to reduce significantly the extent of their disadvantages in the employment field. We quote this example not to denigrate it, but to demonstrate that achieving longer-term changes in offenders' conditions and status may be considerably more difficult than diverting them from arrest and incarceration.

Diversification and decarceration programmes have also been criticized for failing to divert offenders effectively. It has been claimed that many of those 'diverted' were not at risk of prosecution, let alone imprisonment, and might well otherwise have been dealt with informally by the police. Similarly, many of those dealt with by non-custodial sentences would have been unlikely to have been imprisoned for their offences. Thus there is a risk that diversion programmes 'widen the net of social control' – a criticism that has also, as we have seen, been made against police cautioning of juveniles in England and Wales.

Evaluations of these programmes have not always been conclusive in demonstrating their effectiveness. Many schemes have low recidivism rates by comparison with custodial institutions, but it is not always clear whether these were outcomes of the intervention, or simply effects of projects taking offenders with low probabilities of reoffending. More rigorously controlled experiments have tended to show fewer overall differences. Nevertheless, the fact that such projects can show any good results, even if with 'amenable' clients, is encouraging.[28]

We should in any case recognize that the lack of impact of diversion and decarceration schemes is not due solely to the fact that some of them have picked for their target group offenders who do not need them anyway. Another cause may be that these projects are still in the process of developing their methods of working and discovering the most effective ones. One review of diversion and deinstitutionalization of juvenile offenders[29] suggested that the most successful programmes tended to be those that did *not* rely only on the traditional social work methods of casework and counselling, but used such intervention strategies as advocacy, opportunity enhancement and skill development. The New York Court Employment Project serves to warn us, however, that the effectiveness of even these strategies can be limited.

As we have suggested in the context of the Massachusetts experiment, staff too can often, intentionally or unintentionally, subvert, delay or modify new initiatives and so limit their impact. It may be, therefore, that, while a gradualist approach is more common than reform by edict (as in Massachusetts), it is also less likely to be successful unless it is monitored carefully to ensure that it is achieving its objectives of changing the way the criminal justice system treats offenders.

Finally, in this brief summary of foreign examples of alternatives to custody, we should look also at the system of juvenile justice used in Scotland.

Scottish procedures are significantly different from those which exist in the rest of the United Kingdom. In 1964 the Kilbrandon Committee proposed the establishment in each local authority of a Children's Panel made up of lay members of the community. It was to be the job of panel members, who would sit in groups of three, to consider the cases of children brought before them who seemed to be in need of 'compulsory measures of care'. It was proposed that the police, social workers, or any other interested party would be able to refer a child to a Reporter, who would then decide whether or not any action was necessary. If the Reporter decided that some action had to be taken, he would then arrange for the child to receive informal supervision from a social worker and so divert the child away from the more intensive agents of social control, but he could also bring the child before a Hearing. Where innocence was claimed, the Hearing would not indulge in matters of proof and adjudication would be left with the Sheriff's Court; the sole purpose of the Hearing would be to consider the best interests of the child. The proposals were incorporated into the Social Work (Scotland) Act 1968 and came into effect in April 1971. The Kilbrandon Committee had proposed that the panels would consist of people with specialist knowledge and experience, but the 1966 White Paper *Social Work and the Community* wanted to make the panels representative of the whole community. Most of the people who sit on the panels do, in fact, have some experience of working with children in a professional capacity, but a small number of 'outsiders' are involved.

The same conflicting philosophies of justice and welfare which we have seen in the operation of the 1969 Children and Young Persons Act are evident in the Scottish experience. Although no distinction is made between the procedures for dealing with a child who has committed an offence and one who is judged to be in need of care and protection, the conflict between the emphasis on the need to protect society while providing for the welfare of the child has not been resolved. The Hearings can impose quite severe penalties, including the commitment of children to what are now List D schools and which were previously 'approved schools'. They can also 'discharge the referral' or order social work supervision (with or without other conditions); supervision requirements must be renewed at least every twelve months. As the Hearings' actions are conceived to be 'in the best interests of the child', they lack some of the coercive power of courts. In particular they cannot impose fines or order (although they can persuade) the juvenile to make reparation for the offence.

Since the Children's Hearing system has been operating in Scotland it has been reported that the juvenile crime rate has fallen since 1974[30] – although the existence of the Hearing system, with no clear distinctions between offences and other deviant behaviour, makes such statistics difficult to collect – and that the number of juveniles receiving custodial sentences or residential supervision requirements fell during the 1970s.[31] In the latter trend Scotland appears to have been more like other Western European countries where the use of custody for juveniles has not risen to the extent that it has in England and Wales.

Clearly then, it seems that a reform such as that arising from the Kilbrandon Report can be adopted in such a way as to divert young offenders from custodial and residential institutions without adversely affecting the juvenile crime rate. How far this change is the result of the adoption of the Hearing system, and how far it is a consequence of other, unexplained, changes is not obvious but, as the Hearing system is the most salient element of the new regime, logic suggests that it should take the main share of the credit.

The failure of American deinstitutionalization and diversion programmes to make a consistent impact on the use of custody, however, does suggest that amendments to the system need to be monitored carefully and implemented thoroughly if they are to achieve their objectives. Thus we may suspect that the importation of the Kilbrandon system into England and Wales would not *of itself*, however desirable it may be as a reform in its own right, reverse the present tendency to use custody ever more frequently as a response to juvenile offending.

Despite these warnings, we can conclude this chapter on an optimistic note. The experiences of other jurisdictions in dealing with offenders may show us that there is no universal solution, but they also demonstrate the advantages that can come, firstly, from diverse rather than limited programmes and, secondly, from the adoption of sentences that take more notice of the rights of victims and offenders to self-determination. Within the English and Welsh contexts the sentences available that come closest to this model are probation and supervision orders, community service by offenders and deferred sentences, but other more radical approaches may also need to be developed alongside them.

NOTES AND REFERENCES

1 T. Pickles, 'The Chinese Connection', *Community Care*, No. 426, 1982, pp. 16–17.

2 C. Fitzmaurice and K. Pease, 'Prison Sentences and Population: A Comparison of Some European Countries', *Justice of the Peace*, Vol. 146, 1982, pp. 557–9.

3 See T. Weigend, 'Continental Cures for American Ailments: European Criminal Procedure as a Model for Law Reform', in N. Morris and M. Tonry (eds), *Crime and Justice*, Vol. 2, Chicago and London: University of Chicago Press, 1980, pp. 381–428.

4 Ibid.

5 I. Antilla, 'Correction in Finland', in R.J. Wicks and H.H.A. Cooper (eds), *International Corrections*, Lexington and Toronto: Lexington Books, 1979, p. 107.

6 L. Hulsman, 'Penal Reform in the Netherlands: Part II – Criteria for Deciding on Alternatives to Imprisonment', *Howard Journal*, Vol. 21, No. 1, 1982, pp. 35–47.

7 See Howard League for Penal Reform, *Freedom on Licence*, London: Howard League, 1981, pp. 41–9.

8 See Home Office, *Youth Custody and Supervision: A New Sentence*, HMSO, 1978.

9 C. Fitzmaurice and K. Pease, 'Prison Sentences and Population', op. cit.

10 Home Office, *Criminal Statistics, England and Wales 1980*, London: HMSO, 1981. Swedish statistics are taken from *Kriminalvarden 1978*, pp. 20–21.

11 The low prison population in the Netherlands has often been cited as an example we should follow, but, as we have seen, this appears to have been achieved at the expense of a high rate of custodial sentencing.

12 In the USA probation orders can have conditions such as community service added to them. Other sanctions, such as fines, can rarely be used for serious cases.

13 Including health and social services.

14 B. Coates, D. Miller and L.E. Ohlin, *Diversity in a Youth Correctional System: Handling Delinquents in Massachusetts*, Cambridge, Mass.: Ballinger, 1978.

15 See Chapter 3 and also M. Wright, *Making Good: Prisons, Punishment and Beyond*, London: Burnett, 1982.

16 C.A. Murray, D. Thomson and C.B. Israel, *UDIS: Deinstitutionalizing the Chronic Juvenile Offender*, Washington DC: American Institutes for Research, 1978.

17 Ibid., pp. 65 and 93–4.

18 See, for example, ILPAS, *Adventure Activities*, London: ILPAS, 1981, and ILPAS, *The Basement: A Report on Hammersmith Day Centre*, London: ILPAS, 1977.

19 C.A. Murray *et al.*, *UDIS*, op. cit.

20 See W.J. Reid and A.W. Shyne, *Brief and Extended Casework*, New York: Columbia University Press, 1969; W.J. Reid and L. Epstein, *Task Centered Casework*, New York: Columbia University Press, 1972; and W.J. Reid, *The Task Centered System*, New York: Columbia University Press, 1978.

21 C.A. Murray *et al.*, *UDIS*, op. cit.

22 T. Palmer, 'The Youth Authority's Community Treatment Project', *Federal Probation*, Vol. 38, No. 1, 1974, pp. 3–14.

23 P. Lerman, *Community Treatment and Social Control: A Critical Analysis of Juvenile Correctional Policy*, Chicago: University of Chicago Press, 1975.

24 L. Hulsman, 'Penal Reform in the Netherlands', op. cit.

26 J.S. Palmer, 'Pre-Arrest Diversion: Victim Confrontation', *Federal Probation*, Vol. 38, No. 3, 1974, pp. 12–17.

27 NILECJ/LEAA, *Instead of Jail: Pre and Post Trial Alternatives to Jail Incarceration*, Vol. 3: *Alternatives to Prosecution*, Washington DC: US Department of Justice, 1977.

28 S.J. Gerhold, *A Functional Analysis of Four Community Based Juvenile Correctional Programs*, unpublished dissertation, 1980.

29 M.W. Klein, 'Deinstitutionalization and Diversion of Juvenile Offenders', in N. Morris and M. Tonry (eds), *Crime and Justice*, Vol. 1, Chicago and London: University of Chicago Press, 1979, pp. 145–201.

30 *NACRO Briefing*, October 1981.

31 Ibid.

32 DHSS, *Offending by Young People*, London: DHSS, 1981.

Chapter Nine

THE WAY FORWARD?

Before we enter a discussion about the ways in which alternatives to custody can be used to reduce the number of offenders sentenced to prisons, we shall attempt to set a context for this discussion by examining some relevant features of the criminal justice system as it operates in this country.

The first of these is the relationship between sentencing and offending. It is assumed that the sentencing of offenders can be evaluated in terms of the extent to which they are reconvicted, and we have used this measure ourselves in our argument. Reconviction rates as a measure of outcome have been criticized, but surveys such as the Cambridge Study in Delinquent Development have shown a strong association between official and self-reported delinquency sufficient to uphold reconviction as a measure of outcome for adult offenders at least.[1] Furthermore, as Folkard has observed, studies have shown that improvements in what might be called offenders' 'social functioning' appear to be associated with reductions in their propensity to reoffend—in other words that schemes which succeed in helping offenders are also likely to produce lower reconviction rates.[2] For these reasons we accept the value of reconviction as a measure of outcome, while recognizing that it has its limitations, and needs to be validated continually by being set against other, less official, indicators of success or failure. We can agree further that different sentences can, *in theory*, lead to differing reconviction rates with different groups of offenders—a proposition which receives empirical support from Walker's reanalysis of the Home Office's six-year follow-up study of convicted offenders.[3]

Most of the material we have discussed so far in this chapter has been based on what might be called the 'natural' reconviction rates arising within a fixed period from each sentence, irrespective of whether that sentence is one of custody, supervision or restraint in the community, or one involving no restraint at all. Walker, in his article, specifically discounted the incapacitating effect of prison by *increasing* the reconviction rates of prisoners, according to the length of sentence, to include offences they might be presumed to have committed had they not been 'inside'. Thus, most reconviction studies implicitly, and Walker's reanalysis explicitly, measure what might be described as the 'reformative' or 'deterrent' (from future offending) effects of sentencing.[4]

It is clear, however, that custodial sentences can in theory also reduce reconviction rates merely by keeping offenders out of the community, so that they are denied the opportunity to commit any further crimes. Thus custodial sentences can have an 'incapacitative' effect as well as those of reformation and deterrence.

The proposition that sentencing can, in various ways, affect the future criminal behaviour of its subjects therefore seems well grounded, and it seems a logical step to suppose that it can, by incapacitating, reforming or deterring offenders, affect the overall level of crime in society. Indeed, the present Government's policies towards offending stem from the Tory Party's identification of law and order as an issue in the 1979 election, and it must be presumed that they are informed by a belief that what the courts do has some impact on the crime rate, in addition to any 'moral regeneration' that the Government's social and economic policies might achieve.[5]

This view, that sentencing policy can affect the crime rate, has been given weight by the finding that a substantial proportion of solved crime is committed by recidivist offenders. With the apparent discrediting of 'treatment', and the development of arguments for 'justice' in sentencing, there has grown up an argument that one of the proper functions of sentencing is to protect the public from violent crime specifically by the imposition of severe, incapacitating, custodial sentences on those who do, or might, commit such crimes. This has resulted, in America, in several propositions that the mandatory imposition of a prison sentence (usually three or five years) for any felony (roughly similar to an indictable offence in England), or for violent offences, would significantly reduce the crime rate.

The theory of this argument was tested in the USA by the Academy for Contemporary Problems using data from the criminal records of Franklin County, Ohio,[6] to discover how many of those arrested for violent offences in 1973 would have been restrained by various policies of incapacitation (i.e. three- or five-year prison sentences for any serious offences (felonies) or just for violent offences). From this the authors, Van Dine, Conrad and Dinitz, went on to calculate the overall effect of incapacitation on the crime rate. The conclusions they came to were that only an insignificant amount (4 per cent) of violent crime in 1973 could definitely have been prevented had those offenders with previous convictions for felonies received five-year prison sentences for their earlier offences. One reason for this was that those arrested who had previous records of felonies had committed only a small proportion of the violent offences reported to the police. The project also estimated the *likely* prevention rates, on various assumptions about who committed the 70 per cent of violent crimes that were not cleared up (i.e. attributed to an arrested defendant) by the police, of such a policy of automatically imposing a five-year prison sentence for *any* felony conviction. It was calculated that *at most* about a third of the violent offences reported to the police could have been prevented by this sentencing policy at the cost of increasing the prison population to *five times* its current level. The authors of the project report concluded that the savagery of such a sentencing policy was not justified by its likely effect on the crime rate.[7]

This conclusion is a valuable corrective to comments such as Farrington's that, if the incapacitation effects are *included* in assessments of effectiveness,

> . . . prison sentences might prove to be more effective in reducing offending by convicted persons (at least against members of the public) than non-institutional sentences. In order to find no difference, there would have to be a dramatic increase in offending after release from prison to compensate for the dramatic decrease which occurs while the offender is incarcerated.[8]

From our point of view, however, the reasons for the results of the Franklin County study are at least as important as the findings themselves.

The first reason for the relative ineffectiveness of incapacitation was that a substantial percentage of those arrested for offences of violence were first offenders (who could not have been prevented from offending by an earlier prison sentence). Secondly, there were very few offenders in the sample who made a 'career', as it were, of violent crime. Most of the previous convictions of those arrested for violent offences in 1973 were for non-violent crimes against *property*. Thirdly, these offenders were convicted relatively *infrequently* (over half had gaps of over three and a half years between arrests) and their records, if any, were built up over long periods of time.[9]

The picture that emerges from these observations is *not* of dedicated, frequent, violent offenders; most of the offences for which this American sample were arrested were spontaneous rather than premeditated; most of them were preceded by a miscellany of property offences, or by no serious offence. On this basis the concept of 'career criminals' seems not only inappropriate, but seriously misleading as a description of those who commit crimes of violence, unless one is prepared to believe that two convictions make a criminal career. The rational deduction is that most violent crime is committed by those who are not arrested, or by offenders who have no serious criminal record, and this indeed is the conclusion that Van Dine, Conrad and Dinitz came to in their study. In their estimates of 'probable' and 'reasonable' distributions of violent crime among known and unknown offenders, they came to the conclusion that between 66 and 75 per cent of violent crimes reported in Franklin County in 1973 had been committed by people with *no known previous convictions for felonies* in the previous five years.[10] As their model also suggested that 72 per cent of the reported violent crime could be attributed to those who were arrested, it seems obvious that a sentencing policy of incapacitation can make no significant contribution to reducing violent crime, but that the police, by arresting offenders, and the courts by sentencing them, can do something in response to these offences.

It is, however, a weakness of the model developed in this project that only about half those *arrested* were actually found guilty as charged, and that only about a third of the charges were proven; a disturbing corollary, therefore, of the conclusions above is that the model attributes a significant proportion – between a third and a half – of violent crime to people who were *not* found to be guilty of such an offence. If we assume that those arrested were responsible *only* for the offences of which they were convicted, we must conclude that most violent crime in Franklin County was committed by people who never had been and never would be arrested or convicted for their offences. This observation should remind us first that the model is only a model, and second that the decisions and events in the criminal justice system may bear only a tenuous relationship to the 'real world' of crime.

To us, however, the key finding from this study is that the violent offenders identified did not constitute a readily identifiable hard core of criminals processed through the system, but instead a random selection of first offenders and experienced property offenders whose main characteristics were that they were 'the poor, the black and the disadvantaged'. Thus, while there may be 'dangerous' and violent offenders, their violence cannot be predicted from their criminal records.[11]

These findings are hardly novel ones, in that the association between deprivation and offending has been chronicled in many studies.[12] Belief in 'specialization' by offenders dies hard, however, despite the fact that, as Farrington has noted, longitudinal studies have produced little, if any, evidence to support it.[13]

If 'violent' offences are committed largely by people without a record of violence, then much crime, or at least a substantial proportion of those offences for which a conviction is obtained, is committed by people with short or non-existent criminal records. This means in turn that a large minority of people are drawn into the criminal justice system. Farrington quotes several studies suggesting that, by the age of majority, about a fifth of English males have been convicted or cautioned for an indictable (or 'triable each way') offence.[14] Indeed, nearly a third of the subjects of the Cambridge Study (based on boys from a working-class area of London) had acquired a conviction by their twenty-first birthday. As West observes, in the context of an estimated national prevalence rate of 27 per cent for convictions of those aged up to twenty-five, 'Such a large proportion of the young male population cannot all be seriously maladjusted.'[15]

Equally, however, the majority of those convicted do not reoffend. The Cambridge Study found that most of the first or second offenders in their sample had 'dropped out' of crime by the age of nineteen or twenty.[16] Similarly, the Home Office reconviction survey found that adult first or second offenders were highly unlikely to be reconvicted.[17] Thus, for most offenders, delinquency is a relatively fleeting experience; few persist to become recidivists.

The facts are that a large percentage of the male population acquires a criminal record; that a majority of those who do are not reconvicted, or only reconvicted once after this; and that there is no evidence from their criminal records that the majority of offenders specialize in particular offences. These facts all suggest to us that sentencing measures designed to *reform* and *deter* the guilty are as likely to be ineffective in reducing the crime rate as Van Dine's research has shown policies based on incapacitation would be.[18] Apparently it is not offenders that produce crime, but society that produces offenders – like dragon's teeth. Conversely, reforming, deterrent or incapacitating sentences could be *less* effective than they are today *without* significantly increasing the crime rate.[19]

It follows from this that the only effect sentencing policy can have on the crime rate is to deter people from ever offending. As custodial sentences become more frequent, however, so the crime rate increases, providing no evidence that punitive sentencing has any general deterrent effect. Indeed it has become a truism that the perceived likelihood of being caught is in general a better deterrent than the likely sentence.

If sentencing policy has no effect on the crime rate, then it can only be directed towards individual offenders, to reform, deter, incapacitate or punish them as a consequence of their offence. This may seem a trite or obvious point to any reader with some expertise in this area, but it is one that may be obscured by rhetoric about, for example, the war against crime. If Governments are ever tempted to adopt legislation based in part on the theory of incapacitation demolished by Van Dine, Conrad and Dinitz, this obvious point should perhaps be restated more forcefully in other contexts.

We have already referred to the converse of the proposition that 'incapacitation' doesn't work; namely that fewer offenders could be sent to prison, or that offenders could serve shorter sentences without appreciably increasing the risks to society from an increased crime rate. A study by the Home Office Research Unit in 1980[20] estimated, using a methodology similar to Van Dine's, the effects of three different sentencing policies – a mandatory minimum of an eighteen-month prison sentence, an increase in remission from a third to a half the sentence, and a reduction of all custodial sentences by four months – for 'serious' (that is indictable or serious non-indictable) offences. The authors of the report, Stephen Brody and Roger Tarling, came to two distinct conclusions. Firstly, that the imposition of mandatory eighteen-month sentences for 'serious offences' would have prevented between a fifth and a quarter of convictions for such offences, by incapacitating convicted offenders for a year, but only at a cost of a seven-fold increase in the population of custodial institutions. Conversely, a policy of reducing sentence lengths would have increased the number of convictions by only between 1 and 2 per cent and reduced the prison population by between 25 and 40 per cent.[21] It should be noted that these estimates are necessarily based on the assumption that changing sentence lengths will have no effect on other aspects of the criminal justice system – such as the rate at which suspected offenders are brought before the courts – and in any case they only cover changes in the numbers of *convictions* recorded. A further estimate needs to be made of the effects on the crime rate.

This Brody and Tarling attempted, if not in any detail. They concluded, from the findings of Belson[22] and West and Farrington[23] that the most criminal juveniles were also the ones most likely to be convicted, and that a high proportion of recorded crime (and presumably a greater percentage than that 'cleared up' by the police) was in fact committed by persons who were subsequently convicted of an offence. They therefore commented that changes in sentencing policy are 'likely to have a greater impact on overall levels of crime than indicated by analyses limited to convictions'.[24] Put more specifically, this appears to mean that a seven-fold increase in the prison population could achieve a fall of over a quarter in the crime rate, while the cost of a 25 or 40 per cent reduction in the number of prisoners would be rather more than a 2 per cent increase in the number of offences.

In fact these propositions are only doubtfully true. The fact that a certain proportion of the population are both frequent offenders and more likely to be convicted does not necessarily mean that this group is responsible for a disproportionate amount of crime. The Franklin County study we have referred to stemmed in part from similar research findings (that a 'dangerous few' young people were particularly likely to commit violent offences), yet it discovered that much violent crime was attributable to first offenders or those with no previous record of violence.[25] Similarly, therefore, the fact that in England and Wales frequent offenders are apparently more likely to be convicted does not necessarily mean that *their* incarceration would lead to a significant decrease in the crime rate.

In any case, the 'crime rate' itself is by no means such a clear-cut measure as we might naïvely think. While it is generally accepted that the actual level of crime is higher than the numbers of offences recorded each year, it is tacitly assumed that trends in these statistics do represent real changes in society's experience of crime. When one looks more closely behind the figures, however, these changes become more elusive and less easy to see or measure. The *General Household Survey*, for example, failed to find any significant change in the number of households burgled between 1972 and 1980, although it found that the percentage of these burglaries reported to the police over this period rose from 72 per cent to 81 per cent. Over the same period, however, the number of corresponding offences recorded by the police rose by 27 per cent.[26] This discrepancy can partly be accounted for by changes in the readiness of victims to report crimes to the police, but it also appears to stem from the ways the police themselves *record* crimes reported to them.

Richard Sparks found, in a pilot survey of victimization rates in Inner London, that only about two-thirds of the crimes that victims claimed in the survey had been reported to the police, and that some of these had apparently not been recorded as crimes by the police. Thus, police recording practices appeared to introduce biases into the criminal statistics over and above those induced by differential reporting rates. Overall then, the chances of a particular crime being reported to the police and recorded in the official statistics seem to vary according not only to the type of offence, but also to the area where it was committed. Sparks found, for example, that while the 'actual' crime rates (as claimed by respondents in the survey) in the two London areas of Kensington and Brixton were fairly similar (that in Kensington was 17 per cent higher), the differences between them were exaggerated in the official statistics where Kensington appeared to have 55 per cent more crime than Brixton. Most of this difference stemmed from the ways the police recorded crimes reported to them:

they were roughly 40 per cent *more* likely to record a reported crime in Kensington than in Brixton.[27]

The most significant conclusions (in our view) that Sparks drew from these findings were that relatively small changes in the reporting and recording of crime – and particularly less common crimes such as robberies and assaults – could create exaggerated impressions of a 'crime wave' and that crimes committed in middle-class areas might be more likely to be recorded in the statistics than those in working-class districts[28] – even though working-class people appeared to regard property offences as *more* serious than did the middle classes.[29] Sparks's general findings about the existence of differences between levels of experienced and reported crime have recently been confirmed with the publication of the first report on the British Crime Survey.[30] It is reasonable to conclude that his doubts about the validity of trends in British crime statistics are well founded.

We have spent some time on this problem of crime statistics not because we intend to deny that crime has increased since the Second World War (as opportunities for it have also grown), but because we wish to emphasize again the tenuous relationship between the operations of justice, and particularly sentencing, and the impact of crime on society. Our reason for stressing this in the context of alternatives to custody is that it shows once more how sentencing can affect the individual offender, but have little impact on society.[31]

This is particularly important in a discussion of the development of non-custodial alternatives because it reduces the validity of arguments that invoke custodial sentences to protect society from offenders; the protection gained is less than the risks created through those forces in society that help turn other people to crime. It also suggests that in the 'war against crime' long custodial sentences are an expensive irrelevance.

Many would say, however, that custodial sentences are still appropriate to mark society's disapproval of an offence, both as punishment and as a general deterrent to would-be offenders. It has been accepted that long custodial sentences in fact are no more effective in changing offenders than are short ones;[32] if they are also ineffective in reducing the crime rate then perhaps they should be replaced by shorter sentences.

This would also have the effect of reducing the prison population, as the overcrowding in our prisons stems principally from the lengths of the prison sentences imposed by English and Welsh courts, rather than from the numbers sent there.[33] It has been argued that by cutting prison sentences to the lengths used by courts in Holland, Sweden, or even Scotland, the adult prison population could be reduced to a fifth or a half of its present level.[34] This analysis has been based on comparative figures of prison populations and receptions into prisons in eight western European countries. As we observed in the previous chapter, however, those countries where courts impose relatively short prison sentences are also ones where courts are *more* willing to use prison as a sanction for offences. For example, Holland, with probably the fewest prisoners relative to its total population, has courts that use prison nearly twice as often as do those in England and Wales. Conversely, France, where prison sentences appear, on average, to be nearly twice as long as they are in England, uses them only one-third as often as English courts do; for this reason the French adult prison population appears to be, relatively, the second lowest of the eight European countries.

We should remember, therefore, that the danger implicit in promoting shorter prison sentences is that more offenders will be put in custody, and this danger makes the need for non-custodial sentences as pressing as ever. Thus, while we would not argue against the introduction of shorter custodial sentences, we see them as an irrelevance to our main argument, that non-custodial sentences should be used even more frequently by the courts than they are now. Emptying the prisons through shorter sentences will be a hollow achievement if the courts only fill them up again.

Some at least of the arguments we have deployed against imprisonment apply to non-custodial sentences as well. Even if the latter do deter, contain or reform offenders as efficiently, or inefficiently, as prisons, their impact on the incidence of crimes is as likely to be marginal.

So far, our argument has been to demonstrate the virtual irrelevance of the criminal justice system to the problem of crime in society. Sentencing offenders can only affect the crime rate at ruinous cost. If follows from this that sentences can only be justified in terms of the moral statements they make about offences, their ability to punish or reform *individual* offenders.

There is certainly room in our system for making these expressions of morality more consistent and equitable. Our laws are notoriously less severe on the rich and powerful than on the poor and weak. To take one example of this, businessmen who defraud the Customs and Excise of VAT or import duties worth thousands of pounds are able to buy immunity from prosecution by making reparation for their crimes, while a man who forges a £20 DHSS giro or works while claiming benefit can face a prison sentence or a harsh fine with no comparable opportunities for restitution.[35]

Some sentences, especially fines, weigh inequitably on rich and poor; in setting fines courts are generally supposed to take less account of the offender's ability to pay (although there are exceptions to this) than of the seriousness of the offence. By contrast, many continental jurisdictions have a system of 'day fines', where the amount of the fine is assessed in terms of multiples of the offender's daily wage.[36]

These and other similar examples of structural inequality in the system need to be eradicated before our sentencing policy and practice can be perceived as unequivocally moral. We are left, therefore, with the ability of sentences to punish and reform convicted offenders. The evidence of the inability of custodial sentences to reform offenders has already been amply demonstrated; so too has their ability to punish, but we would argue that there should be limits to that punishment and that, if punishment is necessary, then it should be imposed in the community where possible.

The reformative capacity of non-custodial sentences has also been queried, particularly in the works of Lipton (1975) and Brody (1976), but it is our view that the position that 'nothing works' is an oversimplification.[37]

The factors which lead to offending behaviour are complex and various. The last volume of the Cambridge Delinquency Study reports, D. J. West's *Delinquency: Its Roots, Careers and Prospects* (1982), presents a useful summary of the position as far as we know it. The 'causal pathways to delinquency' West sets out can be listed as follows:[38]

Hereditary disposition
Bad home environment
Delinquent personality

Political and economic forces and social traditions
Membership of minority group
Poor social circumstances
Lack of social opportunities

Crime-prone person
Precipitating events
Opportunities for crime

The first three elements roughly fit the 'treatment model' for offenders, on the assumption that intervention can change or ameliorate the effects of these causes that lie in the delinquent's background. The next four are less amenable to individual intervention and belong in the wider realm of political action to remove deprivation, prejudice and their effects. The last three elements are those which appear in the scheme West presents to be closest to the offence itself.

Action to reform delinquents from further offending needs to operate in all three areas to be effective. Traditionally, the approach of treatment has concentrated on the offender's self and his background. Current probation practice appears to focus more on factors associated with the events precipitating the crime, and thus on immediate problems rather than on more distant causes.[39] This in turn leads probation officers to attempt to provide some, if only limited, remedies to deeper-rooted 'structural' problems – unemployment, homelessness and poverty. In moving away from the classical model of treatment, probation officers have followed the same trend of practice as other social workers.

As the aims of social work intervention thus become less focused on the client's existential situation, so there is a need for the methods to become more diverse. 'Traditional' individual casework or counselling, unless explicitly linked with intervention strategies focused on problems,[40] may well be inappropriate to meet these current aims of helping offenders. Methods such as advocacy and various forms of education and training (including social skills) may be more useful. One critique of diversion and deinstitutionalization programmes for juveniles[41] suggests that those projects which used more diverse methods, and put relatively less emphasis on counselling and casework, were more likely to be successful.

The point of this is to show briefly that the current methodologies of intervention by social workers are not so far distant from the needs of clients as some critics of treatment would have us believe. Furthermore, the general case for the ineffectiveness of social work has been weakened by more recent findings that suggest positive associations between intervention and outcome.[42]

Thus the potential exists for probation officers, and other social workers, to help their clients to avoid further convictions. This potential may be increased in relation to one factor that West's taxonomy does not, perhaps, stress fully: the deviant lifestyle. The American sociologist, David Matza,[43] argued that deviancy (and thus, by extension, delinquency) was to a large extent the result of conscious choices rather than unconscious promptings. Once a person had chosen to move towards deviance, so events and influences in their life could be seen as confirming (or undermining) their deviant self-image.

This bald summary can hardly do justice to Matza's argument; what is important from our point of view is the significance his theory gives to outside influences confirming or undermining a chosen lifestyle. We have already noted (in Chapters 2 and 3) the relevance of this to the development of intermediate treatment schemes. The theories that can be seen to underlie such programmes can be seen as cases or corollaries of Matza's more general theory of deviancy in that giving delinquents the opportunity to experience non-delinquent events and lifestyles (if only briefly) may have the effect of reinforcing the non-deviant aspects of their self-image and undermining the deviant elements. Again, this seems to reinforce our contention that supervision of offenders in the community, with the opportunity for diverse forms of practice, still gives courts a significant opportunity of passing sentences *to reform* individual offenders.

At this point in the argument we return to focus on the sentences currently available to the courts, to attempt to see where they fit in with our discussions of the purpose and effects of sentencing. We have proposed that sentences can be evaluated only as far as they affect the individual offender, and have characterized that effect as being reformative or punitive. Obviously this is too simple a typology, and we suggest therefore that the non-custodial or semi-custodial sentencing options available to the courts can have different combinations of the following elements:

1) *Warning* against the consequences of future behaviour, as in probation orders, conditional discharges and deferred sentences, all of which allow the court to resentence for the original offence *if* the defendant reoffends while the order or period of deferment is still current.

2) *Threatening* a (further) prison sentence for reoffending. In fully and partially suspended sentences, the prospect of a prison sentence is more immediate than in 'warning' sentences; the main objective of the sentence is to convey and enforce this threat to ensure 'good behaviour'. Parole, remission and supervised after-care also contain 'threatening' elements.

3) *Controlling* the offender's behaviour for a period, and within limits. The four sentences which involve some form of supervision by probation or social services – Children and Young Persons Act supervision orders, suspended sentence supervision orders, probation orders and community service orders – all *control* offenders in varying degrees, by requiring them to report to a supervising officer or to work under supervision. In a probation order this control can be extended to monitor the offender's accommodation and employment. Attendance centres also come into this group.

4) *Reforming* the offender. The word 'reform' is used here to embrace not only 'treatment', but also more general forms of social work help, the concept of 'reform by example' contained in the community service order and reform by changing status

(e.g. finding a job). All but one of the reformative sentences (probation, community service order, the supervision orders and the deferred sentence) are controlling as well, if only in that reform is presumed to take place as a result of contact with the supervising officer (or doing work in the case of the community service order). The one exception is the deferred sentence, which envisages the possibility of 'self-reform'. It is interesting to note that attendance centres, originally punitive and controlling, have developed and are developing programmes that are also reformative in intent.

5) *Enabling restitution* by the offender. Only the deferred sentence contains the idea that this restitution might be made directly to his victim by the offender, and then only as a possibility. Community service contains the idea of a generalized restitution to society by the offender.
6) *Punishing* the offender. All those sentences which *control* offenders contain a punitive element, in that they involve restricting offenders' liberty, either in relatively trivial ways by requiring them to report to a probation officer or social worker, or seriously, as in community service orders. In these controlling orders, except for community service and attendance centres, the main objective is to *help* the offender, although the correlates of this help may be seen as punitive, unequivocally so in the case of the Kent Control Unit. By contrast, fines and the partially suspended sentence are *wholly* punitive sentences with few, if any, other characteristics.

The proliferation of multi-faceted alternatives to custody that our criminal justice system now boasts has unfortunately failed to reduce the prison population. This now stands at over 45,000, the highest this century, and even the recent tentative trend towards shorter prison sentences appears to have halted.

Government policy appears to offer the following principal remedies:

For young offenders – an extension of community service to sixteen-year-olds, presumably as an alternative to detention centre sentences; and more scope for the use of kinds of intermediate treatment in supervision orders (in addition to an open invitation, in the Youth Custody and Detention sentence, for courts to send many offenders inside for 'short, sharp shocks').

For older offenders – the availability of more explicit and alas perhaps more restrictive conditions in probation orders, and some changes in the parole system.

We have already discussed the types of sentence this legislation represents. It seems to us, however, that these proposals represent, if not the end, than at least an important junction of the road that sentencing policy has been following here over the last two decades. The formal abandonment of treatment as an aim of sentencing, the emphasis on regulatory and diversionary *sentences*, and a new attempt to limit judges' discretion, have all reached a point beyond which it is difficult to see any further initiatives to reduce the numbers in and sent to prison within the present framework of policies and practice.

We therefore need to take stock, to try to establish whether the sentences now available *can* be used to reduce the courts' use of custody, or whether a new approach is needed to the problem.

The first point to stress is that the sentences introduced in the late 1960s and early 1970s specifically as *alternatives* to custody have failed to achieve that objective, although they have now established their own positions in the hierarchy of sentences up to custody. At least half of those given suspended sentences or community service orders would not have received a prison sentence had these 'alternatives' not been available. It seems probable that any new alternatives to custody or indeed any new 'high tariff' sentences would share the fate of these two in that they would be applied half the time to offenders who would otherwise have received less serious sentences. Thus any further pursuit of the policy of alternatives would have as its most likely effect the 'crowding' of the top of the tariff with a variety of sentencing options, and only achieve a partial diversion from custody. A further consequence of the introduction of a new alternative might be to force some existing sentences further down the tariff, so that they become used for less serious offences, or less persistent offenders, than before. Such a process may be seen in the apparent ousting of probation orders by community service, despite the fact that these two options have been structured by the probation service to apply to different kinds of offenders.[44]

If, therefore, the provision of *new* alternatives to custody may be counter-productive, we are left with the choice of developing the use of existing sentences, or suggesting ways of diverting offenders completely from the criminal justice system.

Existing sentences do, in fact, give the courts many opportunities to punish or reform offenders, and these could be exploited more. Community service, it has been argued, has a considerable potential as a punitive alternative to custody; the difficulty with this is that its punitive aspect may often be in conflict with its more uplifting elements – reform by example or experience, and reparation. From the courts' point of view, the latter may be less important, but their de-emphasis could make the operation of these orders by the probation service more problematic. The National Association of Probation Officers, for example, has criticized concentration on the 'disciplinary aspects' of community service and 'the loss of sight of its original positive aims of re-integrating offenders and improving their self-image'.[45] This conflict between the reformative and punitive aspects of community service needs to be resolved soon, if it is to continue to act as a sentence courts can use instead of prison.

For a time the probation order appeared to have been given up as a lost cause, even by Chief Probation Officers.[46] In the last two or three years it has experienced something of a renaissance, although the courts' increased use of probation has probably owed more to the growth in the number of cases they have had to deal with than it does to changes in their views about its value relative to other sentences. We have discussed (in Chapter 4) the reasons behind the recent decline of the probation order, and we have argued that the apparent retreat by probation officers from a practice based in theory on the ideology of treatment has damaged the credibility of probation as a 'high tariff' alternative to custody for more serious offences. On the other hand, the movement away from the classical model of treatment in probation orders seems to us to have led not to the development of work within a paradigm of 'helping' the client, but rather to a greater diversity of intervention strategies encompassing treatment, help, education activities and advocacy, to name some but not all. It is certainly the case that the work of probation officers was not as monolithic in method or purpose as our ascription of it to treatment may suggest and it is also true that the growth of different ways of working pre-dates the apparent decline of treatment.[47] Nevertheless, we suggest that the present practices of probation officers owe a great deal to the criticisms that have been made of treatment. They are also a reaction to the recent growth in the numbers of probation orders made, but there is no evidence so far that this growth is making any significant inroads on the courts' use of custodial sentences.

This last point highlights a particular problem of the role of probation in the criminal justice system. The dwindling credibility of 'treatment' appears to be undermining, or at least hindering, the assertion of the probation order's function as an alternative to custody. The observation that other social work methods can act to 'reform' individual clients at least as effectively as treatment or as punitive sentences has perhaps not been put forward or validated as strongly as it might.

We must recognize, however, that this is all part of the process (particularly noted in the case of community service) whereby presumed alternatives to prison have become sentences in their own right.

The particular dilemma with regard to probation is this. We argue that, as the way the criminal justice system deals with individual offenders appears to be only marginally related to the impact of crime on society, sentencing should focus only on the individual offender and his offence. The application of punishment through a custodial sentence is the most extreme reaction the court can make, and should therefore be limited to the most extreme cases. For many offenders, their offending appears to be linked with various forms of deprivation or with recent personal crises and, for these, some more compassionate response might be appropriate. The probation order is a framework within which that response can be made, giving as it does the opportunity for an offender to get help, treatment or assistance which could alleviate the factors associated with his offending, or divert him from crime into more legitimate pursuits. Probation officers have tended to stress the benevolent parts of their work and to minimize, or reject, any attempts to make them explicitly agents of social control. Yet any attempt to promote the probation order as a non-custodial sentence which is not open about the real abilities of probation officers to act in this way *and* as social workers may itself lead to the spread of social control *down* the tariff.

If we have paid so much attention to the probation order in this discussion, it is because we believe that, within the sentencing options open to the courts, it provides, or rather has the potential to provide, the most realistic alternative to custodial sentencing. The eclectic nature of probation officers' responses to their clients' situations is, we suggest, a strength. There is also a weakness, however, in the dual nature of the order – care and control – from which springs the ambivalence of courts and the probation service to a sentence that encompasses virtually anything between the rigid enforcement of the Kent Control Unit to occasional 'helpful chats'. It is not surprising therefore that the debate that we have chronicled in Chapter 4 has been primarily about this issue, nor that we ourselves have been unable to see a resolution to it. All that we can propose is that the position of the probation order as an alternative to prison does depend on how and where in the debate that resolution is achieved.[48]

One of the values of the 'care' approach to probation is that it can facilitate the integration of offenders into the community. Indeed (setting aside probation officers' apparent need to create specialized educational and welfare systems for their clients) there seems no reason why offenders should be segregated, outside prisons, from their peers. Another form of community involvement, which has recently received considerable attention, is found in those schemes and projects that aim to bring offenders back into contact with their victims.

This is not such a bizarre idea as the last sentence might suggest. A substantial proportion of offences are in fact exchanges between people who already know each other; for many victims the law itself offers little if any practical redress (and then only indirectly through the Criminal Injuries Compensation Board). We have already mentioned examples of projects that attempt to capitalize on or compensate for these facts. The Columbus Night Prosecutor's Program was an example of the former, while the use of 'summary hearings' in France appears to owe much to the latter, making the law more immediate.[49] Now Martin Wright, the former Director of the Howard League, has argued that the principles of reparation by the offender to his victim, and of mediation between offender and victim, should be brought into English criminal justice practice.[50] This proposal has the merit of bringing the 'sentencing' of offenders more under the control of victims, and also of involving victims more with offenders. The advantages of this are that, through victims, 'sentencing' is brought back to the community and victims may come to a better understanding of the offender's delinquency. The major *disadvantage* is that, unless the offences involved are trivial or stem from an existing relationship between offender and victim, it is hard to see some victims, particularly those who have been severely shaken by the crime, being entirely willing themselves to enter into such a process (although they might perhaps ask others to act for them).

From our own particular standpoint, we must add that although it has been argued that 'ordinary people' will be less punitive than judges and magistrates, the evidence for this is not clear cut. Taylor, for example, argues that in a socialist 'popular justice system' prison would be abolished as a sanction for 'minor non-violent property offences' because 'popular rhetorics of justice would operate to define the bulk of the offences for which people are imprisoned as offences demanding compensation or other non-segregative responses'.[51] The findings of a preliminary study of victimization in London tend to cast doubt on this assertion, however. The researchers in this study found that their working-class respondents (unless they were frequent offenders themselves) regarded property offences as *more* serious than middle-class respondents (who perhaps suffered less financially).[52] It is possible to write this view off as an example of 'false consciousness' or as a natural by-product of the inequalities of British society. Nevertheless, the fact remains that there is no particular reason to suppose that 'popular rhetorics of justice' would naturally lead to a lower use of prison nor, in the context of Martin Wright's proposal, that victims would necessarily wish to treat offenders less severely than do the courts.

Having said this, we are still left with the belief that Martin Wright's proposal should be adopted, in spirit if not word for word. Our reason for this is that it offers an escape from the fundamental problem of our criminal justice system, its apparent irrelevance to people's experiences of crime.

We have spent some space at the beginning of this chapter demonstrating how little effect sentencing policies appear to have on crime rates, and that, from one perspective at least, crime statistics themselves are in part an artificial construct of the processes by which they are recorded. Neither of these observations is particularly novel, although they have been tested more thoroughly in the last seven or eight years. What has not always been stressed, however, is the damage that they do to utilitarian justifications of criminal policy ('the greatest good for the greatest number') by showing how its consequences apply *only* to the individual offender, and not to society as a whole except perhaps as symbolic activities.

In that the law itself appears to be concerned only with individuals, this need not disturb sentencers unduly, but in any discussion of sentencing practice the issues become essentially and uncomfortably moral ones. As such, they highlight the ambivalent nature of sentencing policy in its attitudes to individuals – is it to control (and punish) them? Or to care for, help (and treat) them?

We have seen often in this book how this ambivalence has inhibited attempts to provide realistic alternatives to custodial sentences, and how it can also lead to a counter-effect: 'the worrying modern trend towards greater social control . . . in pursuit of a transcendent policy of providing "alternatives to custody".'[53] In the long term it seems to us that the only way out of this dilemma is to find ways of making sentencing the property of the victim, as only he or she has the right to determine it. Schemes of mediation and reparation represent one way of doing this while, at the same time, giving the victim responsibilities (by involvement in mediation or reparation) that may be commensurate with these rights.

We must recognize, however, that the immediate chances of such a system being adopted in England and Wales are small, although we would hope that at least some movements could be made towards this goal.

In the meantime, the task remains of finding and using alternatives to custody within our present unreconstructed system of criminal justice. There are in fact only three kinds of sentence that may be seen as strong enough for this purpose, but do not rely on the threat of a prison sentence for their effectiveness (even if custody is used as a sanction to enforce compliance with them). These are fines, community service and supervision through probation or supervision orders. Of these, fines are used most frequently by the courts, but problems with their enforcement (with large fines in particular) tend to limit their value for serious offences, or for offenders too poor to pay.

As we have seen, community service is potentially the most successful of the 'new alternatives'. After nearly a decade it appears to be fitting into the tariff as a serious sentence in its own right, and longer orders at least can be seen as equivalent to shorter custodial sentences. On the other hand, this process may tend to limit the applicability of community service orders to offences even higher up the tariff. For these, therefore, the main alternative to an immediate or suspended custodial sentence must remain the probation order. While the demise of 'treatment' may have moved probation down the tariff, the increasing flexibility in its use may allow it to be moved up, if necessary, at least until better alternatives can be found.

NOTES AND REFERENCES

1 See D.J. West and D.P. Farrington, *The Delinquent Way of Life*, London: Heinemann, 1977, and D.J. West, *Delinquency: Its Roots, Careers and Prospects*, London: Heinemann, 1982. The position for juveniles is more complex than for adults because police discretion in the use of cautioning (see Chapters 2 and 3) may discriminate between otherwise similar young offenders. Even so, the avoidance of reconviction, and therefore a low reconviction rate, can be seen as evidence for the success of programmes for juveniles, even if this results from an increase in police cautioning for the same act, because the evidence suggests that cautioning itself is associated with fewer further offences.

2 M.S. Folkard, 'Second Thoughts on IMPACT', in E.M. Goldberg and N. Connelly (eds), *Evaluative Research in Social Care*, London: Heinemann Educational, 1981.

3 N. Walker *et al.*, 'Reconviction Rates of Adult Males after Different Sentences', *British Journal of Criminology*, Vol. 21, No. 4, 1981, pp. 357–60.

4 Ibid. These can include effects of 'containment', such as the presumed ability of probation officers to delay by supervision, even if they cannot cure, reoffending.

5 This is too complex an issue to cover here; it merits a book to itself. For an analysis, from a Marxist perspective, of right-wing criminology, see I.R. Taylor, *Law and Order: Arguments for Socialism*, London: Macmillan, 1981.

6 S. Van Dine, J.P. Conrad and S. Dinitz, *Restraining the Wicked*, Lexington: Lexington Books, 1979.

7 Ibid.

8 D.P. Farrington, 'Longitudinal Research on Crime and Delinquency', in N. Morris and M. Tonry (eds), *Crime and Justice*, Vol. 1, Chicago and London: University of Chicago Press, 1979.

9 S. Van Dine *et al.*, *Restraining the Wicked*, op. cit., pp. 39–43.

10 Ibid., pp. 118–22.

11 Ibid., pp. 36–40.

12 See D.J. West, *Delinquency: Its Roots, Careers and Prospects*, op. cit., and D.J. West and D.P. Farrington, *The Delinquent Way of Life*, op. cit.

13 D.P. Farrington, 'Longitudinal Research on Crime and Delinquency', op. cit., pp. 303–4.

14 Ibid., pp. 295–6.

15 D.J. West, *Delinquency: Its Roots, Careers and Prospects*, op. cit., p. 14.

16 Ibid., p. 145.

17 G.J.O. Philpotts and L.B. Lancucki, *Previous Convictions, Sentence and Reconviction*, Home Office Research Study No. 53, London: HMSO, 1979.

18 S. Van Dine *et al.*, *Restraining the Wicked*, op. cit. See also T. Palmer, *Correctional Intervention and Research*, Lexington and Toronto: Lexington Books, 1979.

19 S. Brody and R. Tarling, *Taking Offenders out of Circulation*, Home Office Research Study No. 64, London: HMSO, 1980.

20. Ibid.

21 Ibid., p. 17. Some of the 'serious' offences were less serious than others; they included relatively trivial thefts.

22 W.A. Belson, *Juvenile Theft: The Causal Factors*, London: Harper & Row, 1977.

23 D.J. West and D.P. Farrington, *The Delinquent Way of Life*, op. cit., p. 18.

24 S. Brody and R. Tarling, *Taking Offenders out of Circulation*, op. cit., p. 19.

25 S. Van Dine *et al.*, *Restraining the Wicked*, op. cit.

26 Office of Population Censuses and Surveys, Social Survey Division, *General Household Survey 1980*, London: HMSO, 1982.

27 R.F. Sparks, H.G. Genn and D.J. Dodd, *Surveying Victims: A Study of the Measurement of Criminal Victimisation*, Chichester: John Wiley, 1977.

28 Ibid., pp. 155–60.

29 Ibid., pp. 181–90.

30 M. Hough and P. Mayhew, *The British Crime Survey: First Report*, Home Office Research Study No. 76, London: HMSO, 1983.

31 The one group of obvious partial exceptions to this are known violent offenders; several of these, however, have reformed themselves through – or in spite of – their treatment in custody, and even for violent offenders there are no good predictors of dangerousness.

32 See D. Lipton, R. Martinson and J. Wilks, *The Effectiveness of Correctional Treatment: A Survey of Treatment Evaluation Studies*, New York: Praeger Publishers Inc., 1975. Their study also found, however, that *very* long custodial sentences appeared to be as effective in achieving change as very short ones.

33 C. Fitzmaurice and K. Pease, 'Prison Sentences and Population: A Comparison of Some European Countries', *Justice of the Peace*, Vol. 146, 1982, pp. 577–9. In fact this is true only for adult prisoners; juvenile courts have become increasingly ready to impose custodial sentences (see Chapter 2).

34 Ibid., p. 579. This of course applies only to adult *sentenced* prisoners, who comprise about 55 per cent of the total prison population.

35 See 'Notes of the Week: Compounding the Prosecution', *Justice of the Peace*, Vol. 145, No. 37, 1981, p. 542.

36 See 'Fining the Rich', *Justice of the Peace*, Vol. 146, 1982, pp. 364–5.

37 D. Lipton *et al.*, *The Effectiveness of Correctional Treatment*, op. cit., and S.R. Brody, *The Effectiveness of Sentencing*, Home Office Research Study No. 32, London: HMSO, 1976.

38 D.J. West, *Delinquency: Its Roots, Careers and Prospects*, op. cit., p. 129.

39 See Chapter 4.

40 See W. Reid, *The Task-Centered System*, New York: Columbia University Press, 1978, and E.M. Goldberg and S.J. Stanley, 'A Task-Centred Approach to Probation', in J.F.S. King (ed.), *Pressures and Change in the Probation Service*, Cambridge: University of Cambridge Institute of Criminology, 1979.

41 M.W. Klein, 'Deinstitutionalization and Diversion of Juvenile Offenders', in N. Morris and M. Tonry (eds), *Crime and Justice*, Vol. 1, Chicago and London: University of Chicago Press, 1979, pp. 145–201.

42 W.J. Reid and P. Hanrahan, 'The Effectiveness of Social Work: Recent Evidence', in E.M. Goldberg and N. Connelly (eds), *Evaluative Research in Social Care*, op. cit.

43 D. Matza, *Becoming Deviant*, New Jersey: Prentice-Hall, 1969; D. Matza, *Delinquency and Drift*, New York: John Wiley, 1964.

44 See Chapter 5.

45 NAPO, *The Provision of Alternatives to Custody and the Use of the Probation Order*, London: NAPO, 1981, p. 7.

46 See House of Commons Fifteenth Report from the Expenditure Committee, Session 1977–1978, *The Reduction of Pressure on the Prison System*, Vol. I, London: HMSO, 1978.

47 See D.A.C. Millard, 'Broader Approaches to Probation Practice', in J.F.S. King (ed.), *Pressures and Change in the Probation Service*, op. cit.

48 Note that we allow for more than one resolution; our criminal justice system is not one that puts a premium on rigid sentencing policies. For one CPO's view as to where the resolution should lie, see W.A. Griffiths, 'Supervision in the Community', *Justice of the Peace*, Vol. 146, 1982, pp. 514–5.

49 See T. Weigend, 'Continental Cures for American Ailments: European Criminal Procedure as a Model for Law Reform', in N. Morris and M. Tonry (eds), *Crime and Justice*, Vol. 2, Chicago and London: University of Chicago Press 1980, pp. 301–428.

50 M. Wright, *Making Good: Prisons, Punishment and Beyond*, London: Burnett, 1982.

51 I.R. Taylor, *Law and Order*, op. cit., p. 141.

52 R.F. Sparks *et al.*, *Surveying Victims*, op. cit., pp. 181–90.

53 W. McWilliams, Review of Beaumont and Walker's *Probation Work: Critical Theory and Socialist Practice*, *British Journal of Social Work*, Vol. 12, No. 2, 1982, pp. 218–19.

Select Bibliography

Adams, R., Allard, S., Baldwin, J. and Thomas, J., *A Measure of Diversion? Case Studies in Intermediate Treatment*, London: National Youth Bureau Publications, 1981.

Advisory Council on the Penal System, *Sentences of Imprisonment: A Review of Maximum Penalties*, London: HMSO, 1978.

Antilla, I., 'Correction in Finland', in R.J. Wicks, and H.H.A. Cooper, (eds), *International Corrections*, Lexington and Toronto: Lexington Books, 1979.

Beaumont, B. and Walker, H., *Probation Work: Critical Theory and Socialist Practice*, Oxford: Basil Blackwell, 1981.

Belson, W.A., *Juvenile Theft – The Causal Factors*, London: Harper & Row, 1977.

Bochel, D., *Probation and After-Care: Its Development in England and Wales*, Edinburgh: Scottish Academic Press, 1976.

Bottoms, A.E. and McWilliams, W., 'A Non-Treatment Paradigm for Probation Practice', *British Journal of Social Work*, Vol. 9, 1979, pp. 159–202.

Brody, S.R., *The Effectiveness of Sentencing*, Home Office Research Study No. 32, London: HMSO, 1976.

Brody, S.R. and Tarling, R., *Taking Offenders out of Circulation*, Home Office Research Study No. 64, London: HMSO, 1980.

Bryant, M., Coker, J., Estlea, B., Himmel, S. and Knapp, T., 'Sentenced to Social Work?', *Probation Journal*, Vol. 25, 1978, pp. 110–14.

Cawson, P., *Young Offenders in Care*, London: DHSS, 1980.

Child, the Family and the Young Offender, The, London: HMSO, 1965.

Children and Young Persons Scotland, Edinburgh: HMSO, 1964.

Children in Trouble, London: HMSO, 1968.

Cloward, R.A. and Ohlin, L.E., *Delinquency and Opportunity*, London: Routledge & Kegan Paul, 1960.

Coates, B., Miller, D. and Ohlin, L.E., *Diversity in a Youth Correctional System: Handling Delinquents in Massachusetts*, Cambridge, Mass.: Ballinger, 1978.

Cohen, A., *Delinquent Boys: The Culture of the Gang*, London: Collier Macmillan, 1955.

Corden, J., Kuipers, J. and Wilson, K., *After Prison: A Study of the Post-Release Experiences of Discharged Prisoners*, University of York Department of Social Administration, Papers in Community Studies No. 21, 1978.

Department of Health and Social Security. *Offending by Young People: A Survey of Recent Trends*, London: DHSS, 1981.

Department of Health and Social Security Social Work Service Development Group, *Intermediate Treatment: Planning for Action*, London: DHSS, 1977.

Ditchfield, J.A., *Police Cautioning in England and Wales*, Home Office Research Study No. 37, London: HMSO, 1976.

Fairhead, S., *Persistent Petty Offenders*, Home Office Research Study No. 66, London: HMSO, 1981.

Farrington, D., 'Longitudinal Research on Crime and Delinquency', in N. Morris and M. Tonry (eds), *Crime and Justice*, Vol. 1, Chicago and London: University of Chicago Press, 1979.

Fitzmaurice, C. and Pease, K., 'Prison Sentences and Population: A Comparison of Some European Countries', *Justice of the Peace*, Vol. 146, 1982, pp. 577–9.

Folkard, M.S. *et al.*, *Intensive Matched Probation and After-Care Treatment*, Vol. I: *The Design of the Probation Experiment and an Interim Evaluation*, Home Office Research Study No. 24, London: HMSO, 1974; Vol. II: *The Results of the Experiment*, Home Office Research Study No. 26, London: HMSO, 1976.

Folkard, M.S., 'Second Thoughts on IMPACT', in E.M. Goldberg, and N. Connelly (eds), *Evaluative Research in Social Care*, London: Heinemann Educational, 1981.

Goldberg, E.M. and Stanley, S.J., 'A Task-Centred Approach to Probation', in J.F.S. King (ed.), *Pressures and Change in the Probation Service*, Cambridge: University of Cambridge Institute of Criminology, Cropwood Conference Series No. 11, 1979.

Goldberg, E.M. and Warburton, W., *Ends and Means in Social Work*, London: Allen & Unwin, 1978.

Goldstone, His Honour Judge, 'A Fresh Look at Community Service Orders', *The Magistrate*, May 1982.

Hardiker, P., 'The Role of Probation Officers in Sentencing', in H. Parker (ed.), *Social Work and the Courts*, London: Edward Arnold, 1979.

Hardiker, P., 'Social Work Ideologies in the Probation Service',

British Journal of Social Work, Vol. 7, No. 22, 1977, pp. 131–54.

Haxby, D., *Probation, a Changing Service*, London: Constable, 1978.

Hine, J., McWilliams, W. and Pease, K., 'Recommendations, Social Information and Sentencing', *Howard Journal*, Vol. 17, No. 2, 1978, pp. 91–100.

Holborn, J., 'Casework with Short-Term Prisoners', in Home Office Research Study No. 28, *Some Male Offenders' Problems*, London: HMSO, 1975.

Home Office, *Criminal Statistics, England and Wales 1981*, London: HMSO, 1982.

Home Office, *Prison Statistics, England and Wales 1982*, London: HMSO, 1983.

Home Office, *Review of Parole*, London: HMSO, 1981.

Home Office, *Youth Custody and Supervision: A New Sentence*, London: HMSO, 1978.

Hough, M. and Mayhew, P., *The British Crime Survey: First Report*, Home Office Research Study No. 76, London: HMSO, 1983.

House of Commons Fifteenth Report from the Expenditure Committee, Session 1977–1978, *The Reduction of Pressure on the Prison System*, Vol. I, London: HMSO, 1978.

Howard League for Penal Reform, *Freedom on Licence: The Development of Parole and Proposals for Reform*, Sunbury: Quartermaine House, 1981.

Hulsman, L., 'Penal Reform in the Netherlands: Part II – Criteria for Deciding on Alternatives to Imprisonment', *Howard Journal*, Vol. 21, No. 1, 1982, pp. 35–47.

Lillyquist, M., *Understanding and Changing Criminal Behavior*, New Jersey: Prentice-Hall, 1980.

Lipton, D., Martinson, R. and Wilks, J., *The Effectiveness of Correctional Treatment: A Survey of Treatment Evaluation Studies*, New York: Praeger Publishers Inc., 1975.

Martinson, R., 'What Works? Questions and Answers about Prison Reform', *The Public Interest*, No. 35, 1974, pp. 22–54.

Matza, D., *Becoming Deviant*, New Jersey: Prentice-Hall, 1969.

Millham, S., Bullock, R. and Hosie, K., *Locking Up Children: Secure Provision within the Child Care System*, London: Saxon House, 1978.

Morris, A., 'Diversion of Juvenile Offenders from the Criminal Justice System', in N. Tutt (ed.), *Alternative Strategies for Coping with Crime*, London: Basil Blackwell & Martin Rochester, 1978.

Morris, P. and Beverley, F., *On Licence: A Study of Parole*, London: John Wiley & Sons, 1972.

Murray, C.A., Thomson, D. and Israel, C.B., *UDIS: Deinstitutionalizing the Chronic Juvenile Offender*, Washington DC: American Institutes for Research, 1978.

Paley, J. and Leeves, R., 'Some Questions About the Reverse Tariff', *British Journal of Social Work*, Vol. 12, No. 4, 1982, pp. 363–80.

Palmer, T., *Correctional Intervention and Research*, Lexington and Toronto: Lexington Books 1978.

Parsloe, P., 'Issues of Social Control', in J.F.S. King (ed.), *Pressures and Change in the Probation Service*, Cambridge: University of Cambridge Institute of Criminology, Cropwood Conference Series No. 11, 1979.

Pease, K., 'Community Service and Prison', in K. Pease and W. McWilliams (eds), *Community Service by Order*, Edinburgh: Scottish Academic Press, 1980.

Pease, K. *et al.*, *Community Service Assessed in 1976*, Home Office Research Study No. 39, London: HMSO, 1977.

Pease, K. *et al.*, *Community Service Orders*, Home Office Research Study No. 29, London: HMSO, 1975.

Philpotts, G.J.O. and Lancucki, L.B., *Previous Convictions, Sentence and Reconviction: A Statistical Study of a Sample of 5,000 Offenders Convicted in January 1971*, Home Office Research Study No. 53, London: HMSO, 1979.

Radzinowicz, L., *The Results of Probation*, London: Macmillan, 1958.

Reid, B., 'The Evaluation of Social Work', in E.M. Goldberg and N. Connelly (eds), *Evaluative Research in Social Care*, London: Heinemann Educational, 1981.

Reid, W.J. and Hanrahan, P., The Effectiveness of Social Work: Recent Evidence', *The Task-Centered System*, New York: Columbia University Press, 1978.

Roberts, J. and Roberts, C., 'Social Enquiry Reports and Sentencing', *Howard Journal*, Vol. 21, No. 2, 1982, pp. 76–93.

Shaw, S., *Paying the Penalty: An Analysis of the Cost of Penal Sanctions*, London: NACRO, 1980.

Sheppard, B., 'Monitoring Two New Approaches in Hampshire', *Justice of the Peace*, Vol. 146, No. 37, 1982, pp. 560–62.

Sparks, R.F., Genn, H.G. and Dodd, D.J., *Surveying Victims: A Study of the Measurement of Criminal Victimisation*, Chichester: John Wiley, 1977.

Taylor, I.R., *Law and Order: Arguments for Socialism*, London: Macmillan, 1981.

Taylor, L., *Deviance and Society*, London: Thomas Nelson/Michael Joseph, 1971.

Van Dine, S., Conrad, J.P. and Dinitz, S., *Restraining the Wicked*, Lexington: Lexington Books, 1979.

Vanstone, M. and Raynor, P., 'Diversion from Prison – Partial Success and a Missed Opportunity', *Probation Journal*, Vol. 28, No. 3, 1981, pp. 85–9.

Von Hirsh, A., *Doing Justice: The Choice of Punishments*, Toronto: McGraw-Hill Ryerson Ltd, 1976.

Walker, N., Farrington, D.P. and Tucker, G., 'Reconviction Rates of Adult Males after Different Sentences', *British Journal of Criminology*, Vol. 21, No. 4, 1981, pp. 357–60.

Walmsley, R., *Steps from Prison*, London: Inner London Probation and After-Care Service, 1976.

Weigend, T., 'Continental Cures for American Ailments: European Criminal Procedure as a Model for Law Reform', in N. Morris and M. Tonry (eds), *Crime and Justice*, Vol. 2, Chicago and London: The University of Chicago Press, 1980.

West, D.J., *Delinquency: Its Roots, Careers and Prospects*, London: Heinemann, 1982.

West, D.J. and Farrington, D.P., *The Delinquent Way of Life*, London: Heinemann, 1977.

West, D.J. and Farrington, D.P., *Who Becomes Delinquent?*, London: Heinemann, 1973.

Willis, A., 'The Balance between Care and Control in Probation: A Research Note', *British Journal of Social Work*, Vol. 13, No. 3, 1983, pp. 339–46.

Wright, M., *Making Good: Prisons, Punishment and Beyond*, London: Burnett, 1982.

Index